Vertically iNclined

Climbing Higher with God

Mary A. Kassian

LifeWay Press®
Nashville, TN

ISBN 0-6330-9525-7

This book is a resource in the Bible Studies category of the Christian Growth Study Plan.
Course CG-1029

Dewey Decimal Classification: 248.843
Subject Headings: SPIRITUAL LIFE\WOMEN\DISCIPLESHIP

Unless otherwise indicated, all Scripture quotations are from the Holy Bible, *New International Version*, copyright © 1973, 1978, 1984 by International Bible Society. Used by permission.

Scripture quotations identified ESV are from the Holy Bible, *English Standard Version*.
© 2001 by Crossway Bibles, a division of Good News Publishers.

Eugene H. Patterson, *The Message* (Colorado Springs, CO: Navpress, 2002)

Scripture quotations identified NKJV are from the *New King James Version*. Copyright © 1979, 1980, 1982, Thomas Nelson, Inc. Publishers. Used by permission.

Scripture quotations identified NASB are from the NEW AMERICAN STANDARD BIBLE, © Copyright The Lockman Foundation, 1960, 1962, 1963, 1968, 1971, 1972, 1973, 1975, 1977, 1995. Used by permission.

Scripture quotations identified KJV are from the *King James Version*.

To order additional copies of this resource: WRITE LifeWay Church Resources Customer Service; One LifeWay Plaza; Nashville, TN 37234-0113; FAX order to (615) 251-5933; PHONE (800) 458-2772; E-MAIL to *customerservice@lifeway.com*; ORDER ONLINE at *www.lifeway.com*; or VISIT the LifeWay Christian Store serving you.

Printed in the United States of America

Leadership and Adult Publishing
LifeWay Church Resources
One LifeWay Plaza
Nashville, TN 37234-0175

Contents

About the Author

Looking back, I'm amazed at how much we packed into that old brown station wagon. The canvas tent, camping gear, and suitcases were carefully fit like a jigsaw puzzle on the roof, covered with a tarp, and roped to the rack. My dad occupied the driver's seat, while my mom sat on the far side of the front bench. My little brother and his favorite blanket were tucked in the small space between. I remember noticing how his little runners bobbed on the end of his outstretched legs—like exclamation marks in the textbooks I was leaving far behind.

On the passenger floor, around her feet, Mom kept several bags. The most important overflowed with apples, sandwiches, drinks, and other eating supplies. Beside that, her huge, oversized purse bulged with hankies, scissors, collapsible tools, pens, band-aids, twist ties, and dozens of other items that she thought might be useful. Another bag was jammed full of assorted books, magazines, and maps. A final bag lay empty, awaiting the garbage that six kids were sure to produce.

In the back of the station wagon, my two oldest brothers sat on the pop-up seats facing each other. I was jealous. They were the best seats—the rear window stretched all the way across. They could make the glass go up and down by cranking the metal handle. And they could make faces at the people in the cars behind. But being second youngest, and the only girl, I had to sit over the hump on the middle bench, a brother on each side. It wasn't very comfortable, but that wouldn't bother me for a while. As the low-riding vehicle backed out of the driveway, I was merely overcome with excitement. It was vacation time! We were going to the mountains!

Mary

Mary Kassian was born and raised in Edmonton, Canada. She and her husband, Brent, have three sons: Clark, Matthew, and Jonathan. Mary has mastered the art of cheering after spending countless hours in rinks, arenas, and gyms: her husband is chaplain for a professional football team, her two older sons play ice hockey, and her youngest, volleyball. The Kassians enjoy biking, hiking, snorkeling, music, board games, mountains, campfires, and their family's black lab, General Beau.

Mary has studied rehabilitation medicine and systematic theology. She is author of several books, Bible studies, and videos, including *In My Father's House: Women Relating to God as Father* and *Conversation Peace: The Power of Transformed Speech*. In this resource, Mary takes us to her favorite place—the Rocky Mountains of Canada—to explore what it takes to climb higher with God.

Seven Summits

At age 33, blind mountain climber, Erik Weihenmayer, completed his historic seven summits expedition. Scaling all seven summits—the highest peak on each of the world's seven continents—is the ultimate mountaineering achievement. From the craggy peaks of McKinley and Kilimanjaro to the icy dangers of Everest, Erik had the vision to dream big, the courage to reach for the unseen, and the grit and determination to push for the top of the mountain.

Erik's quest is not unlike the quest of the Godward climber. Climbing higher with God also demands that we have the vision to dream big, the courage to reach for the unseen, and the grit and determination to push for the top. It's a spiritual quest. It's the life-long ambition of pursuing what the Apostle Paul describes as "the upward call of God."

Not that I have already attained, or am already perfected; but I press on, that I may lay hold of that for which Christ Jesus has also laid hold of me. Brethren, I do not count myself to have apprehended; but one thing I do, forgetting those things which are behind and reaching forward to those things which are ahead, I press toward the goal for the prize of the upward call of God in Christ Jesus (Phil. 3:12-14, NKJV).

God is calling you upward—toward Himself. The goal of this study is to help you climb higher. Each week you will be challenged to scale a new mountain. Whether you are just starting off in your journey or are a seasoned climber, ascending these peaks will help you reach the next level with God. Work hard at your lessons! You will find that what you get out of this expedition will be proportionate to the effort you put in. Consider the following suggestions to make your study more meaningful.

- Trust the Holy Spirit to be your teacher. Ask Him for guidance as you seek to learn how to better relate to God and others. Release your mind and heart in ready obedience to all He will teach you.
- Pray sincerely both alone and with others. Base your prayers on what the Holy Spirit has revealed to you through your study.
- Keep a spiritual journal of God's activity in your life as well as your response to Him throughout the study. When God speaks, it is important to record it. Your memory will not always recall these "special moments," but your journal will!
- Live out your growing relationship and knowledge of God in your daily life. Share this freely with others. Be willing to step out of your comfort zone as you climb toward God. Expect God to honor your faithful obedience to Him.

Are you ready for the adventure? Then put on your boots. Let's climb!

About This Study

Welcome to *Vertically Inclined*! By choosing to participate in this study, you are demonstrating your desire to climb higher in your relationship with God. As you complete this study, there are several terms and icons you will encounter each week. Your study will make more sense if you become familiar with these things ahead of time.

Daily Lessons
The daily lessons, to be completed on your own, should take no more than 20 minutes. Each week's lessons will challenge you to ascend a new summit: the Mount of Anticipation, the Mount of Allegiance, the Mount of Appraisal, the Mount of Affliction, the Mount of Affection, and the Mount of Abundance.

Base Camp
At the beginning of each week, participants gather to participate in small-group discussion and to watch a teaching video by Mary Kassian (approximately 25 minutes in length). The video introduces the topic for the week. There's also a summary video session to wrap up the study—that's seven base camp sessions in all. A Base Camp Viewer Guide is included on the second page of each week's lesson. A leader guide is provided on pages 146-152.

Climbing Gear
Every mountaineer depends on good climbing gear. The climbing gear in this study will equip you with practical concepts and skills to help you reach the summit. Gear up whenever you see the symbol.

High Points

Stop and take a look at some of the peaks and valleys mentioned in Scripture: Carmel, Zion, Gerizim, Ebal. From the well known to the lesser known, High Points scope out the spectacular scenery and fascinating significance of these and other historic biblical sites.

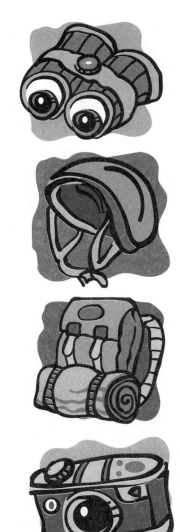

Viewpoints

A lot of people have said good things about climbing mountains. Viewpoints contain gems of mountaineering wisdom from noted climbers, philosophers, and historical figures. Profound, witty, and wise, viewpoints are sure to inspire you to push for the top.

Memory Pack

Pack the Scripture verse for the week into your memory. Cut-out cards are included on page 159 so you can carry the verse in your purse or pocket.

Photo Album

Vertically Inclined was filmed on location in the spectacular Rocky Mountains. Enjoy the scenery and meet the crew in the team's photo album.

There's one last important bit of information to keep in mind as you study *Vertically Inclined*. The High Points and Climbing Gear sections are designed to supplement your study and can be read as time allows. These sections are in shaded boxes so as not to "interrupt" the flow of the study. Don't let them confuse you. Instead, you can skip over the box and continue with the content of the day's study. But don't forget to come back and check these out!

The Mount of Anticipation

Godward Climbers Anticipate an Encounter with Christ

an•tic•i•pate—To look forward to, to expect, await, eagerly yearn for, to foretaste or foresee. Do you anticipate God? The goal of this week's study is to challenge you to eagerly anticipate God's presence and power in your day-to-day life.

Base Camp
In the Civil War Battle for Chattanooga, the Union and Confederates both knew that capturing Lookout Mountain was vital to success. Jesus taught that being on the lookout is also vital for those who want to succeed spiritually. Godward climbers not only watch for the Big "C"—coming of Christ—they also watch for all the little "c"—comings that are woven into the fabric of the everyday.

Daily Lessons
Day 1: Gaze at the Majesty of the Mountains
       … Anticipate the Maker of the Heights
Day 2: Feel the Mountains Tremble
       … Anticipate the Shaker of the Heights
Day 3: Hear the Call of the Mountains
       … Anticipate Being Drawn to the Heights
Day 4: Watch for Signs on the Mountain
       … Anticipate a Stirring on the Heights
Day 5: Prepare for a Mountain Meeting
       … Anticipate an Encounter on the Heights

High Points
- Mountains and Hills
- Mount Sinai
- Mountain Symbolism
- Mount of Olives
- Mount Moriah

Climbing Gear
- The Secret of Observation
- Keeping Watch

Memory Pack
"Yes, LORD, walking in the way of your laws, we wait for you; your name and renown are the desire of our hearts" (Isa. 26:8).

The Mount of Anticipation: On the Lookout

Luke 12:35-40

This Base Camp Guide will help you follow the video session for Summit 1.

Introduction: Lookout Mountain—It's important to be on the lookout.

1. God is always on the move.

a. He _____.

b. He provides _____ of _____.

2. God moves in surprising ways.

a. In _____ ways

b. In _____ ways

c. In subtle, _____ ways

3. God moves for those who anticipate Him.

a. He _____ for those who _____.

b. He _____ for those who _____.

c. He exceeds our _____ _____.

Be on the lookout for God at all times. Watch for His movements—move when He moves. That's the way to conquer the Mount of Anticipation.

9

Gaze at the Majesty of the Mountains...

Anticipate the Maker of the Heights

Vertically Inclined

"I lift up my eyes to the hills—where does my help come from? My help comes from the Lord, the Maker of heaven and earth" (Ps. 121:1-2).

I am what my mountain-dwelling friends refer to as a "flat-lander"—I live in the prairies, with terrain as flat as a freshly pressed cotton shirt. But every summer, when the sweet clover hangs thick in the sun-kissed air and the fields of canola turn bright saffron, I pack up my boots and bike to heed the call of the mountains. It's a call I cannot ignore. I hear it whisper when the purple crocus first pokes its head through the melting snow. It grows louder and more insistent with each advance of spring. By the time the children are released for vacation, the twinge of longing has intensified into a persistent ache. I don't know when the mountains first gripped me, but they have staked their claim on my heart like a sold sign on the front lawn of a house.

On the appointed day, we direct our vehicle westward. Two hours into our journey, shoots of the Rockies begin to pierce the horizon. They grow to staggering heights. Reunited, my old friends surround and embrace me, and compel me to look up. I think that's the reason I love them. Mountains beckon me to gaze skyward, and, somehow, that helps put everything in perspective. In the clear air, I brush aside the sticky cobwebs of complexity to consider the simple, most profound truths of life. The majesty of the mountains leads me to consider "the Majesty"—the Maker—of the mountains. And I am filled with wonder and awe.

Lift Your Eyes Up

When he was a shepherd, King David, the writer of psalms, made a habit of lifting his eyes up to the mountains. David found that gazing upward put things into perspective. It helped clarify matters in his mind.

According to Psalm 121:1-2, what did David think of when he looked up at the mountains? (Check one.)
❏ God's throne was on the top of the mountain.
❏ The mountain would be the best escape route from his enemies.
❏ God, the Maker of heaven and earth, would help him.
❏ God would supply his troops with water from the mountain spring.

The Bible version you are using may use the term *hills* instead of *mountains*. In the Bible, the terms are often used interchangeably. To find out why, read today's High Point.

Making a Mountain out of a Molehill (Mountains and Hills)

Mountain can be defined as a mass of land rising above the surrounding area. The biblical term for *mountain* can refer to a single mount, a mountain range, or a tract of mountainous terrain. A closely related term (Heb. *gib*, Gr. *bounos*) is normally translated "hill." It's a general term that refers to any elevated site, slope, or ascent. Its root meaning is "bowl" or "hump-backed." In English, we use the term *mountain* or *hill* according to the altitudinal height of the mass of land in question—mountains are thought to be much higher than hills. But in the Bible, the difference is more subtle, and the two terms can be used almost interchangeably. Thus, in the King James translation of the Bible, Jesus is described as ascending the "mount" of transfiguration, but is subsequently described as coming down the "hill" (Luke 9:28-36).[1] Linguistically, biblical authors can make a hill out of a mountain, but we still ought not make a mountain out of a molehill.

The grandeur of the mountains led David to contemplate the Maker of the mountains and the help David could anticipate from Him. The Hebrew word for *make* refers to a deed or work. When used of God, the word emphasizes God's personal involvement in the act of creating. It stresses one of the most basic theological concepts about God. In relationship to His creation, God is both *transcendent* and *immanent*.[2] Those big words represent important ideas to understand. The *transcendence* of God means He is over, above, and beyond (separate from) His creation. Quite simply, it means, "He is bigger than me, and way beyond my reach." The *immanence* of God indicates He is "with" or "alongside" His creation. He participates, on an ongoing basis, in the course of history and in people's lives. *Immanence* means: "God is very near. He is interested and involved in my life. He cares for me."

> "In some way or other the mind is overturned by their dizzying heights and is caught up in contemplation of the Supreme Architect."—Conrad Gesner[3]

Transcendence and Immanence

The concepts of God's *transcendence* (He's bigger than me) and *immanence* (He cares for me) go together like lightning and thunder. David saw the connection clearly. He knew that the God who had the power to make the mountains also had the power, and the interest, to help him in his personal circumstances. In Isaiah 40, the prophet came to the same conclusion.

Read Isaiah 40:12-22, concentrating on verse 12 to complete the labels on the diagram on page 12.

11

He measures the waters in His	He holds the dust of the earth in a	He marks off the heavens with the breadth of His	He weighs the hills and mountains on a
_____	_____	_____	_____

Do these verses speak of God's ❑ transcendence or ❑ immanence?

Isaiah was contemplating the incomparable power and knowledge of God. Humans, nations, and man-made gods amount to nothing when compared to the Almighty Creator. Isaiah was speaking of God's transcendence.

Read Isaiah 40:25-31. The stars demonstrate God's transcendence (v. 26). But notice what Isaiah concludes about God's immanence (His nearness and care). How did Isaiah anticipated the power and strength of God would impact his life?

_____

_____

Isaiah anticipated that God would give him strength and power whenever he felt weary or weak.

Briefly describe a time when you sensed the immanence of God.

_____

_____

Throughout Scripture, you and I are encouraged to observe the handiwork of the Maker of heaven and earth. That's because seeing how big and powerful He is (transcendence) ought to lead us to anticipate His involvement in our lives (immanence). When you look at nature, do you make the same connection? Sharpen your skills of observation with today's Climbing Gear.

The Secret of Observation

David was certain God loved and cared for him personally. His psalms are overflowing with accolades about God's heart: "Great is your love toward me!" (Ps. 86:13). "Your love is ever before me!" (Ps. 26:3). "By day the LORD directs his love, at night his song is with me" (Ps. 42:8). How could David be so sure? What was his secret?

David made a habit of observing and contemplating God's creation. From this, he learned about the love of God. He said, "Great are the works of the LORD; they are pondered by all who delight in them" (Ps. 111:2). And he gave us this gem of advice: "Whoever is wise, let him heed these things and consider the great love of the LORD" (Ps. 107:43).

According to David, truths about God's character are illustrated in nature: the starry heavens show that God's love for us is bigger and higher than we can fathom; the faithful cycle of the sun and moon demonstrate his trust-worthiness; the mountains point to his rock-solid character; the ocean-depths speak of his justice. (Ps. 36:5-6).

Do you make a habit of observing creation and contemplating what it points to? Today, enjoy the majesty of some part of God's creation—a mountain, tree, flower, sunrise, sunset—and consider what it demonstrates about God. Try to be observant, like David. "Lift your eyes up!" Look at what God has made (His transcendence) and ponder how it speaks of His involvement in your life (His immanence). Jot your thoughts in the margin.

> "He throws open the gates of his mountains as a gardener opens the gates of his garden. The heights are a splendid setting for his work."—Gaston Rébuffat[4]

Anticipate the Maker

The prospect of going to the mountains never fails to excite me. I long for the mountains, look for the mountains, antici-pate the mountains. And they do not disappoint. Every year their majesty thrills me.

As we begin our trek up the seven summits of this study, I would like you to consider this question: Do you anticipate God? Do you long for Him, look for Him, and expect that He will use His power and might to do wonderful things in your life? The Maker of the mountains longs to be involved with you on a very personal basis. I guarantee that as you anticipate Him, the beauty of His power and majesty will thrill you.

What I observed in creation today (God's transcendence):

_____

_____

_____

What I concluded about God's involvement in my life (God's immanence):

_____

_____

_____

13

Vertically Inclined

Feel the Mountains Tremble...
Anticipate the Shaker of the Heights

When I was a little girl, I loved thunderstorms. Living in the dry climate of the prairies, we'd only get a few good ones each summer. But as soon as the bolts began to pierce the sky, I'd quickly collect the feather comforter from my bed, the braided floor mat from the back porch, a cookie and glass of milk from the kitchen. Then I'd slip outside to the front steps of the house. In my opinion, it was the best vantage point. Adjacent to the painted wood siding, a narrow, dry strip of concrete created by the overhang of the roof provided shelter. There I'd sit for hours to watch the show.

The sheer beauty and power of lightning fascinated me. The crackling strokes would split the inky canopy with jagged scars, or light up the expanse in quick succession, like a child playfully flicking a switch in a darkened room. Then I would begin to count—"1-one thousand" … "2-one thousand" … "3-one thousand" … until interrupted by the thunderous rumble that inevitably followed. I could never quite remember how many miles were represented by each second's delay, but in my mind, the fewer the better. I was thrilled when a monstrous flash and thunderclap were close enough—and powerful enough—to shake the ground beneath me.

My brother didn't share my fondness for lightning. While I was outside reveling in the display, he was inside cowering in the closet. Had I felt threatened, I would have hid too. But tucked in my little nook, I felt quite safe. Snug, secure, and confident that the storm would not harm me, I was able to delight in its fearsome wonder.

Tremble, Quake, and Shake

The first time I can remember being frightened by a lightning storm was during a campout in the mountains. During the night, the tent we were in was nearly overturned by the ferocious wind. Vainly we struggled to stabilize the aluminum poles to keep them from bending. Rain pelted the flimsy nylon and streamed in through every small opening. Lightning flashed perpetually. And the thunder … never had I heard such thunder! The very foundations of the mountains seemed to shake.

Describe a time you were frightened by the power displayed in nature.

_____

_____

The power displayed in severe storms, hurricanes, tornadoes, and floods is frightening. I was terrified that night in the mountains. But when the storm ended, the mountains were still standing. The power of the mountains was greater than the power of the storm.

Mountains are powerful, but how do mountains stand up to the power of God? Draw lines to match the phrase with the correct reference.

Psalm 18:7	They melt like wax.
Habakkuk 3:6	They tremble and smoke.
Psalm 104:32	They crumble and collapse.
Psalm 97:5	They tremble, quake, and shake.

The power of God is incredible! In His presence, even the mighty mountains melt. When God addressed the people of Israel from Mount Sinai, the mountain burned, smoked, and shook violently (Ex. 19:9-20). Find out more about Mt. Sinai in today's High Point.

> "Henceforth the majesty of God revere; Fear Him, and you have nothing else to fear."
> —James Fordyce (1720-1796).[5]

There's a Whole Lot of Shaking Going On (Mount Sinai)

Horeb is a mountain district in northwest Arabia, on the Sinai Peninsula, where the Israelites arrived three months after they left Egypt. *Horeb*, also called *Sinai*, means "waste" or "dried-up ground." Most scholars identify Mount Sinai with a range of mountains called Jebel Musa (Mount Moses). It's a huge block of mountains about two miles long and one mile wide with a spacious plain at its northeast end, called the Er Rahah, in which the Israelites encamped for nearly a whole year.

Sinai is extremely significant in the history of God's people. Here Moses encountered God in the burning bush (Ex. 3:1-12), obtained water from the rock (Ex. 17:6-7), and received the Ten Commandments (Ex. 20). The Israelites made a covenant with God here (Deut. 5:2), and from here they set out for Canaan, the land He promised them (Deut. 1:19). Later on, the prophet Elijah fled to Sinai to escape Queen Jezebel's wrath (1 Kings 19:8).

Structurally, a huge cliff, known as the Ras Sasafeh, rises almost perpendicularly from the Er Rahah. This protruding bluff is visible against the sky from end to end of that plain, like a huge altar in front of a congregation. This is likely where the people stood, at the base of the mountain, when Moses led them out from the camp to meet with God. Exodus describes the scene for us:

There was thunder and lightning, with a thick cloud over the mountain, and a very loud trumpet blast. Everyone in the camp trembled. Mount Sinai [Horeb] was covered with smoke, because the LORD descended on it in fire. The smoke billowed up from it like smoke from a furnace, the whole mountain trembled violently, and the sound of the trumpet grew louder and louder. Then Moses spoke and the voice of God answered him (Ex. 19:16,18-19).

When God came down, lightning and thunder smashed, a trumpet-sound blasted, smoke billowed, and the mountain shook. The people quaked in fear at the awesome display of power that accompanied God's presence. When God comes near, His power shakes things up. He may "shake" things differently for you than He did for the Hebrew people, but you will not fail to notice His presence. If you ask Him, the Shaker of mountains will come "shake up" your world, and you will be awed by His transforming power.

The people were terrified at the mighty power of God's presence. Some were so frightened that they pleaded for God to stay at a safe distance and speak to them through prophets instead of face-to-face (Deut. 5:4; 18:16-19). But others longed for God to make Himself known. David petitioned, "Summon your power, O God; show us your strength" (Ps. 68:28). Moses begged God to reveal His glory (Ex. 33:18). Isaiah pleaded with God to "rend the heavens and come down!" Read Isaiah 64:1-4 in the margin.

Use the verses from Isaiah 64 to complete the crossword puzzle.

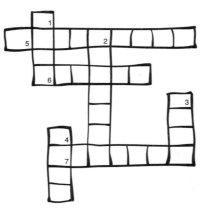

DOWN
1. **What did Isaiah want God to do?**
2. **What do the mountains do before God?**
3. **What does God make known to His enemies?**
4. **What must we do for God to act on our behalf?**

ACROSS
5. **What trembles before God?**
6. **What did the people not do?**
7. **What type of things did God do?**

Refer to the same verses to fill in the blanks of the following sentences.

"Oh, that you would rend the heavens and come down, that the mountains would tremble before you! ... come down to make your name known to your enemies and cause the nations to quake before you! For when you did awesome things that we did not expect, you came down, and the mountains trembled before you. Since ancient times no one has heard, no ear has perceived, no eye has seen any God besides you, who acts on behalf of those who wait for him" (Isa. 64:1-4).

When God comes, He shakes things up. He does things that are

_____ and _____ .

God acts powerfully on behalf of those who _____ for Him.

Did you complete the sentences? You may have said something like, "When God comes, He shakes things up. He does things that are awesome and unexpected. God acts powerfully on behalf of those who wait for Him."

How do you feel about God using His power to do awesome and unexpected things in your life? Check all that apply.

❏ **Ambivalent**—"I don't think about it too much."
❏ **Lackadaisical**—"I'm not interested in Him shaking things up."
❏ **Intimidated**—"I want to keep God at a safe distance."
❏ **Fearful**—"I think He's going to hurt me."
❏ **Skeptical**—"I wonder if He really has that much power."
❏ **Unconvinced**—"I don't think He'll use His power on my behalf."
❏ **Hopeful**—"Maybe He'll do something for me."
❏ **Eager**—"I'm anticipating it!"
❏ **Desperate**—"I fervently and constantly long for it."
❏ **Other:** _____

Power to Shake Your World

Several years ago, during a summer storm, I poured a mug of coffee and headed for the front porch. I wasn't the first one there. My son was sitting on the steps, cocooned in a blanket, watching the show. I sat beside him in silence as we gazed with wonder at the awesome display of God's power.

"Eternity is in the heart of man filling him with longing. But we know not what we long for until we see the breathtaking God." —John Piper[6]

God's power is both wondrous and fearful. The thunderous power displayed in the heavens is but a faint whisper of Him. I ask myself whether I believe—and can even begin to comprehend—that God wants to use this incomparably great power on my behalf and on your behalf. He wants to "shake" our worlds and do awesome and unexpected things in our lives.

Close today's lesson by reading and meditating on Ephesians 3:20-21. Ask the Lord to give you a greater sense of anticipation about what He wants to do in your life over the next few days, weeks, and months.

Summit 1—

The Mount of Anticipation

"Now to Him who is able to do above and beyond all that we ask or think—according to the power that works in you—to Him be glory in the church and in Christ Jesus to all generations, forever and ever. Amen" (Eph. 3:20-21).

17

DAY 3

Hear the Call of the Mountains ...
Anticipate Being Drawn to the Heights

The highest mountain in the world is Mount Everest. In the spring of 1996, the world's attention was directed towards Everest when 12 climbers died attempting the summit. It was not the first time the mountain had claimed lives. From 1921 until then, the peak had been attempted 630 times and the death toll stood at 144—a fatality ratio of almost 1 in 4.

Death on Everest was not unique. Climbers were well aware of the risks. But on this particular occasion, a reporter had been invited along to write about the expedition. Afterwards, from the vantage point of a survivor, he poignantly documented the entire drama. In addition, an IMAX movie team happened to be filming on the mountain during the very time the disaster took place. Because of these two factors, the general public learned about the 1996 tragedy. Such information would have normally been confined to the mountain-climbing community.

The tragedy captured the imagination of millions of people. Jon Krakauer's book, *Into Thin Air*, remained on the New York Times best-seller list for an astounding 56 weeks. The Everest IMAX movie shattered all records. The question that piqued such interest, and fascinated the common flat-lander, was simply the question, "In the face of such danger, why would anyone want to climb the mountain?"

"Because it's there!" was George Mallory's famous retort when a badgering reporter posed the same question in the early 1920s.[8] Shortly after his first Everest attempt, Mallory offered a better explanation. His answer alludes to the lure that grips the heart of the mountain climber, and—as we shall soon see—the lure that inspires the Godward climber to keep pressing upward in pursuit of God.

Upward and Forever Upward

Mallory, the son of a British clergyman, believed that the urge to climb mountains was like the pull of life itself—"upward and forever upward." In other words, there's something in the human soul that instinctively draws us to that which is above and beyond ourselves. Created in the image of God, humans are pulled toward God. Augustine called it the God-shaped vacuum of the heart. The pull that beckons mountaineers to physically climb the mountain can be regarded as symbolic of the pull that beckons people to spiritually climb toward God.

To find out more about the symbolism of mountains, take a look at today's High Point.

More Than Just a Pretty Face (Mountain Symbolism)

Mountains do more than just provide scenery. They are imbued with religious significance and symbolism. You will find numerous Scripture references to the "mountain of the Lord" and to mountains as pictures of God's holiness (Gen. 22:14; Ex. 3:1; Ps. 43:3; Isa. 2:2; Ezek. 28:14; Mic. 4:2; Zech. 8:3).

Mountains figure prominently in contexts of prayer and worship. Worship of pagan deities almost always took place on hilltops and mountaintops (Deut. 12:2; 2 Chron. 21:11). Though Jesus made it clear that the worship of God was not restricted to any particular mountain (John 4:2-24), several mountains are extremely important in the spiritual history of God's people: Mount Sinai, where they received the law and commandments (Ex. 20-34); Mount Gerizim, where they affirmed God's covenant blessings (Deut. 11:29; 27:12; Josh. 8:33); and Mount Zion, where the temple in Jerusalem was located (Ps. 2:6; 78:68; Isa. 8:18). Mount Zion has special significance, as it also refers to the heavenly dwelling place of God (Heb. 12:22; Rev. 14:1).

Mountains also symbolize other concepts. They illustrate overcoming obstacles (Isa. 40:4; Zech. 4:7; Matt. 17:20); strength and victory (Isa. 41:15); and exceeding joy (Isa. 44:23; 55:12). They symbolize protection (Ps. 125:2); righteousness (Ps. 36:6); persons in authority (Ps. 72:1-3); God's kingdom (Isa. 2:2; Dan. 2:35). Scripture uses mountains to picture nations, political/economic structures (Jer. 51:25; Rev. 8:8); proud and haughty persons (Isa. 2:14); and divine judgment (Isa. 42:12-15; Mal. 1:3).

So the next time you see a mountain mentioned in the Bible, remember that mountains present more than just a pretty face. Make sure you keep in mind their spiritual significance and symbolism.

Summit I—

The Mount of Anticipation

"Therefore the LORD longs to be gracious to you, and therefore He waits on high to have compassion on you. For the LORD is a God of justice; How blessed are all those who long for him" (Isa. 30:18, NASB ®).

"Continue seeking Him with seriousness. Unless he wanted you, you would not be wanting Him."
—C.S. Lewis[9]

Read Isaiah 30:18 in the margin and complete the exercises that follow.
- Box the words *longs, waits,* and *long for.*
- Cross out the words *you* and write the word *me* above them.
- Cross out the word *blessed* and write the word *happy* above it.

The verse you just read was from the *New American Standard* ® translation of the Bible. If you have another translation, you may notice that the word *waits* is used in place of the word *longs*. That's because both are translations of the Hebrew word *chakah*, which means "to continue to be in a certain state until an expected event."[10] The word implies a deep desire to see an event occur, coupled with an anticipation that it will, in fact, occur.

19

With this definition in mind, which of the following could be used as synonyms (same meaning) for waits and longs? Put a check beside all the phrases that you think could be used as synonyms.

_____ Longingly desires   _____ Earnestly expects
_____ Confidently hopes   _____ Eagerly anticipates

All of the phrases could be used as synonyms for the Hebrew word *chakah*.

Go back and read Isaiah 30:18 out loud, substituting the phrase "longingly desires" at each place where you drew a box. Do the same thing with all the other phrases. Let the meaning sink in.

On the continuum below, mark an "x" to indicate the extent to which you think God anticipates you.

Not at all   To the greatest extent

According to Isaiah 30:18, God is anticipating you. He longingly desires, earnestly expects, confidently hopes, and eagerly anticipates that you will climb towards Him. The height of the heavens above the earth can't even begin to compare to how much He loves you and longs for you (Ps. 103:11). Did you put a mark on the far end of the scale indicating that God anticipates you "to the greatest extent"?

What are your thoughts when you realize that God has such a great longing for you?

_____

_____

Read the following verses and draw lines to match each reference with the thought that verse contains.

Hosea 11:4   He draws us with loving-kindness.
Jeremiah 31:3   He draws us with cords of kindness and ties of love.
Romans 2:4   His kindness draws us toward repentance.

In the phrases above, highlight or underline the words *draws us*.

The Hebrew word *mashak* is translated as "draw" or "lead." The word literally means: "to cause an object to make linear or vertical movement."[11] God's loving-kindness exerts a pull on us. It draws us upward—toward Him.

On the scale below, indicate the extent to which you feel the pull to climb Godward.

Not at all   To the greatest extent

Just Sheer Joy!

Our longing for God is a response to the longing God has for us. He beckons us from on high. Our joyful anticipation of Him motivates us to climb. Do you feel the pull? Are you a Godward climber? Is the allure of climbing toward Him so great that you can't

"The allure is so great. I must go on. I don't think I could live without climbing."—Christian Bonington, Himalayan Climber[12]

live without climbing? Do you longingly desire, earnestly expect, confidently hope for, and eagerly anticipate Him—as He does you? Close today's lesson by asking the Lord to increase your ability to feel that upward pull. For I believe that you will find, as Mallory did, that "What we get from this adventure is just sheer joy!"

DAY 4
Watch for Signs on the Mountain...
Anticipate a Stirring on the Heights

Vertically Inclined

"My soul waits for the Lord more than watchmen wait for the morning, more than watchmen wait for the morning"
(Ps. 130:6).

Our black lab dog, Beauregard, is highly attuned to the sound of keys. He comes bounding at the slightest jingle—eagerly anticipating a ride in the car. Beau's attitude towards keys can be described by the Hebrew word *chakah*, the word we studied in yesterday's lesson. The word is most often translated "waits." Beau waits for the jingle of keys. Do you remember the four synonyms for the word *waits*?

Try to fill in the blanks from memory. If you need help, refer to yesterday's lesson.

To "wait" means to longingly d __ __ __ __ __, earnestly e __ __ __ __ __,

confidently h __ __ __ and eagerly a __ __ __ __ __ __ __ __ __ __.

The first summit the Godward climber seeks to scale is the Mount of Anticipation. To anticipate God means to approach each day with an attitude of expectancy. It means I desire, expect, hope, and anticipate He will "show up." Like Beau waits for the jingle of keys, I wait for God. I'm not certain how or when He'll move, but I'm confident He will. So I keep watch.

King David is a great example of someone who eagerly anticipated God's presence and power. Every day, David expected God to act. He remained alert and attuned so that he might discern God's slightest movement.

Read Psalm 130:6 in the margin. In the frame below, illustrate or explain how David watched for God.

David anticipated God more than watchmen anticipate the morning. Can you come up with another analogy? I've provided a couple examples.

More than my dog anticipates the jingle of keys.
More than climbers anticipate the mountain.

More than _____

One of the watchtowers of David's city was located on top of the Mount of Olives. Read more about this lookout in today's High Point.

On the Lookout (Mount of Olives)

The Mount of Olives is a mile-long range of four summits that dominates the landscape east of Jerusalem. Because of its elevation, the Mount of Olives functioned as Jerusalem's watchtower. The northern section of the range was called *Scopus*, which means "lookout." Every approach toward the city was visible from this vantage point. Here, the Jews lit signal fires to announce the beginning of worship festivals. A chain of beacons all the way to Mesopotamia transmitted the signal, ensuring that Jews living in other nations could also observe the festivals.

When the radiance of God's presence (the *Shekinah*) departed from the temple because of sin, it was said to linger on the Mount of Olives, waiting for the people to repent (Ezek. 10:18; 11:23).[13] Some have suggested that the Mount of Olives was the place Satan took Jesus to show Him the kingdoms of the world (Matt. 4:8; Luke 4:5). It was the place where Jesus ascended to heaven (Acts 1:6-11); and the place where He will return (Zech. 14:4). Jews believe that those buried on the Mount of Olives will be the first to be resurrected when the Messiah comes.

The base of the Mount of Olives was thickly wooded with olive trees. That's how it got its name. One area of the mount was called *Gethsemane*, which in Hebrew means "oil press." It was a garden area where the olive fruit was processed (John 18:1). Jesus often prayed in that place (Matt. 26:36; Mark 14:32; Luke 22:39-46). It was there He prayed on the night of His betrayal, instructing His disciples to also "keep watch" in prayer (Matt. 26:30-45).

The Mount of Olives is symbolic. It illustrates the concept of "watching for God." Here, the Jews watched for the beacons to signal times of worship. Here, their ancestors failed to watch for God's lingering presence. Here, the disciples watched Christ ascend into heaven and were instructed to watch for His return. Here, Christ modeled what it means to watch for God when He prayed to His Father.

The Mount of Olives is a lookout, and it reminds us to be on the lookout for God, anticipating His presence and involvement in our lives.

"They wait thy presence—eye and heart, With straining gaze and bated breath."—Henry William Herbert[14]

Watch for Him

Jesus often stressed the importance of watching for His coming. But why would He encourage His followers to be on the

23

lookout for an event that wasn't going to happen until long after they died? I believe He encouraged them to watch every day because Christ "comes" every day. One day He will physically return to earth, but He weaves "comings" into the fabric of the everyday.

Jesus knows that those on the lookout for Him at all times—anticipating His movement every day—are ready for His return. Spiritually, they will have seen Him come all the time, so naturally they'll be able to recognize Him when He comes physically. Watching for the little comings prepares us for the Big "C" coming. That's why it's so important to remain on the lookout.

Jesus told numerous parables to stress the importance of being on the lookout. Read the passages below. Draw a line to match each parable's reference with its correct symbol and title.

Reference	Symbol	Title
"Be always on the watch, and pray" (Luke 21:29-36).		The homeowner and the faithful servant
"What I say to you I say to everyone: 'Watch!' " (Mark 13:32-37).		The bridesmaids (virgins)
"Therefore keep watch ... be ready!" (Matt. 24:42-44).		The sprouting fig tree
"Therefore keep watch" (Matt. 25:1-13).		The homeowner and the thief

These parables teach that to be on the lookout for Christ requires a constant attitude of spiritual expectancy (watch) and preparedness (be ready).

In the margin, explain what you think this might involve for you.

He Comes to Those Who Watch

Jesus taught that those who watched would be rewarded, and those who didn't would miss out. The bridesmaid who was prepared enjoyed the wedding feast with the groom; the one who wasn't went hungry. The homeowner who remained on the lookout kept his home safe; the one who didn't was robbed. The person who watched for signs of summer enjoyed the fruit of the fig; the person who didn't missed the whole season.

My favorite among today's parables is the one about the homeowner and the faithful servant. For the Jew, a master returning from a wedding banquet was a classic example of something unpredictable. Jewish weddings were great and elaborate occasions that lasted for days. The celebration would not begin at a specific time, but when all was ready. Therefore, guests could not predict the day and time they would return home. The servant had no idea when his master would come. Nevertheless, he was waiting and ready.

The parable has an extraordinary ending. The master rewarded the expectant servant by doing the unthinkable. He had the servant recline in an easy chair while he went into the kitchen. The master put on an apron and prepared an unbelievable feast. Then, the master served the servant!

The message is clear: Christ comes to those who expect Him to come—to those who are watchful. And when He comes, He does the unexpected. Are you on the lookout for Him? Do you anticipate His coming? Put on today's Climbing Gear to help you "keep watch." Ask the Lord to help you be constantly on the lookout for Him.

"Thou art the star for which all evening waits."
—George Sterling[15]

Keeping Watch

In biblical times, simple watchtowers were built in pastures to protect cattle and sheep against wild animals, and also in vineyards or cornfields to protect crops against thieves. Towers of a more complex structure were incorporated into city walls, as part of a city's defense works (2 Sam. 18:24; Song of Songs 5:7). Watchmen—sentries—were posted in the watchtowers. It was their responsibility to remain alert and on the lookout for any hostile action. City watchmen were also responsible to give word to the king of messengers approaching the city wall (2 Sam. 18:24-27; 2 Kings 9:17-20). Unfaithfulness in the discharge of a watchman's duty was punishable by death (Ezek. 33:6). In times of conflict or hostility, the dangers of the night were especially feared, and watchmen eagerly looked forward to the break of day (Isa. 21:11).

David waited for the Lord as watchmen wait for the morning (Ps. 130:6). Just as watchmen were certain of the coming of dawn, and stayed alert, awaiting it, so David was certain that God would come, and expectantly looked for Him. Do you watch for God as diligently as David did? Do you look for "God-moments" every day? Do you expect God to "come"?

Watch for your next "God-moment." After it happens, record it in the margin. Be prepared to share it at your next base-camp session.

DAY 5
Prepare for a Mountain Meeting ...
Anticipate an Encounter on the Heights

Vertically Inclined

"How lovely is your dwelling place, O LORD Almighty! My soul yearns, even faints, for the courts of the LORD; my heart and my flesh cry out for the living God" (Ps. 84:1-2).

My husband, Brent, is chaplain for a professional CFL Team.[16] During the season, he spends quite a bit of time on the sidelines watching the team practice. One of his favorite drills is the "ball movement" drill. All the offensive linemen (the big, tough guys who protect the quarterback and running backs) and all the defensive linemen (the big, tough guys on the opposite side who try to tackle the quarterback and running backs) line up in their rush or blocking stances. Muscles tensed, they wait in anticipation. The coach, with a football in hand, then begins a spasmodic routine. He twitches and jerks his body every-which-way while he barks out the quarterback count: "Yellow-72; Yellow-84 ... Hup ... Hup!" But only on occasion does he actually move the ball. This simulates the center "snapping" the ball to the quarterback and signals the linemen to spring into action.

Why does the team do this drill? The coach wants his players to anticipate the ball's movement. When the ball moves, they move. Not before, as they will be penalized, and certainly not after, as the opposing team will beat them off the line. Offensive and defensive linemen cannot be distracted by anything else. They need to keep their focus on the ball.

The drill illustrates the point of this week's study. Godward climbers anticipate an encounter with Christ. Their focus is on Him. They are prepared to move when they see Him move. Just as football linemen are assured that the "snap" will indeed happen, likewise, Godward climbers know that their anticipation will not be in vain. Christ will come. He will move. He will meet with those who long for an encounter with Him!

Looking for a Meeting
King David is a good example of someone who longed for an encounter with God. He languished: "As the deer pants for streams of water, so my soul pants for you, O God. My soul thirsts for God, for the living God. When can I go and meet with God?" (Ps. 42:1-2).

Read Psalm 84:1-2 in the margin. Circle the phrases that indicate David longed to meet with God.

The words *yearn*, *faints*, and *cry out* mean to be "totally, completely overcome, spent, and/or consumed with longing." David felt that way about meeting with God. He pleaded, "When can I go to meet Him?" To read more about the place David met with God, read today's High Point.

The Place of Meeting (Mount Moriah)

"The Tent of Meeting" (the tabernacle) was a portable temple structure that accompanied the people of Israel on their journey to their promised homeland. King David set up the tent in Jerusalem after he conquered it. But because the nation had permanently settled into the promised land, he wanted to build a permanent structure—a place where all the people of the nation could go to meet with God.

The site David chose for the temple was Mount Moriah. *Moriah* means "chosen by Jehovah." David encountered God at Moriah during a time of great spiritual crisis (2 Chron 3:1-2). He thus bought the land from a Jebusite who had been using a great rock on its summit as a threshing-floor (2 Sam. 24:24-25; 2 Chron 3:1). It was the place where, in antiquity, Abraham had offered his son, Isaac (Gen. 22:2).

David's son, Solomon, built the first temple on Mount Moriah. But in 587 B.C., a hostile ruler, Nebuchadnezzar, took the Jewish people into exile and virtually destroyed it (2 Kings 25:9-17). Nehemiah rebuilt it 50 years later. For the next few centuries, the temple was the site of various military conflicts and conquests. In 164 B.C., the Maccabees turned the temple into a fortress so strong it resisted the siege of Pompey for 3 months (63 B.C.).

In 19 B.C., in order to win the favor of the Jewish people, King Herod cleared and extended Mount Moriah and began to build a new temple. Herod's temple was a magnificent structure of beautifully cut cream stone, elaborate carvings, and gold ornaments. It was the temple used by the Jews during the time of Christ. It was barely finished before Roman soldiers destroyed it in A.D. 70. Today, an Islamic shrine called "Dome of the Rock" stands on Mount Moriah.

The Greek word for *temple* (*oikos*) means, "house." It is where God dwells. God promised to dwell in His temple forever (Ex. 15:17-18; 1 Kings 6:12-13; Ps. 132:13-14). The physical structure that "housed" His presence has been destroyed for centuries. But the New Testament makes it clear that because of Jesus, a physical structure is no longer needed. God continues to dwell in His temple. It is not a temple made with hands (Acts 7:47-48). Instead, it is a spiritual place. It exists in the hearts of all those who, through Jesus, have entered into a relationship with Him (1 Cor. 3:16; 2 Cor. 6:16; Eph. 2:20-22).

"Come, Lord, come, for without You no day or hour is happy; without You my table is without its guest, for You alone are my joy."—Thomas Á Kempis[17]

The gospel of Luke tells us of two individuals who, like David, were filled with longing to meet God. Read Luke 2:25-38.

What were Simeon and Anna constantly on the lookout for?

❑ The person who would console Israel
❑ The Lord's Christ
❑ The person who would redeem Jerusalem
❑ An impoverished young couple who had a baby out of wedlock
❑ An infant named after the biblical hero, Joshua

Simeon and Anna were on the lookout and had been for many years. They were watching for the Big "C" coming of the Lord's Christ, which God had promised through the prophets. They were looking for the one who would bring consolation and redemption to the Jews. At the time, the Jews believed He would be a political hero who would reestablish Israel as an independent, theocratic nation, free from the rule and oppression of Rome. Did you check the first three boxes?

Simeon and Anna had no idea the Lord's Christ would come in the arms of an impoverished young couple, rumored to have had a baby out of wedlock. They had no idea He would be named Jesus—the Greek form of the Hebrew name, Joshua. They had no idea the kingdom He would establish would first and foremost be a heavenly one. They had no idea He would be crucified as a criminal, and through His blood bring consolation and redemption to all who believed in Him. Christ did not come in the way they thought He would, but they recognized His coming nonetheless.

Simeon and Anna were alert and prepared. They recognized Christ when He came. Yesterday, we learned that being on the lookout for the little "c" comings of Christ is what prepares us to recognize His Big "C" coming.

In the passage you read, what indicates that Simeon and Anna were attentive to the daily little "c" comings of God?

Simeon and Anna were attentive to the small comings of God long before they saw Him come in the flesh. Simeon listened to the revelation of the Holy Spirit. He moved when the Spirit moved. The passage describes him as "righteous" and "devout." The former indicates he dealt with the sin in his life on an ongoing basis, while the latter indicates he earnestly sought God. The passage tells us Anna worshiped night and day. She fasted and prayed. We know she was in the habit of listening to God, because she is described as a prophetess. Simeon and Anna had been on the lookout for a long time when they saw Christ come. They recognized Him because they had nurtured the habit of looking for God every day. Every day they watched and waited.

Waiting is active, not passive, behavior. Active waiting goes hand-in-hand with prayer (Col. 4:2) and obeying the Bible (Ps. 130:5), as well as listening and responding to the Holy Spirit (Gal. 5:25). It involves trust (Ps. 39:7), confidence (Mic. 7:7), patience (Ps. 37:7), and perseverance (Ps. 27:14).

What can you do to actively increase your anticipation of God? Write your thoughts in the margin.

God has promised to reward those who earnestly seek Him (Heb. 11:6) and to act on behalf of those who wait for Him (Isa. 64:4). Those who seek will undoubtedly find. He's given His word. "As surely as the sun rises, he will appear; he will come to us like the winter rains, like the spring rains that water the earth" (Hos. 6:3).

"Come Lord Jesus!"

Maranatha is one of the few Aramaic words that the first-century Greek-speaking church preserved from the language of Jesus. It means, "Our, Lord, Come!" (1 Cor. 16:22). Early believers used the word often. It expressed their daily anticipation of Jesus. Though Christ did not physically return in their lifetime, their longing did not go unanswered. God gives us glimpses of what we passionately want to see. As we yearn, and long, and look for Him, He will come!

"Do you think it all meant nothing, all the longing?
… All my life the god of the Mountain has been wooing me."—C.S. Lewis[18]

To complete this week's trek up the Mount of Anticipation, reflect on what God taught you this week. You may want to look back over the lessons to refresh your memory. Read the quote by Á Kempis on page 27 and reread Psalm 84:1-2 in the margin. In the margin or on a separate sheet of paper, write a prayer expressing your personal longing for Christ.

"How lovely is your dwelling place, O LORD Almighty! My soul yearns, even faints, for the courts of the LORD; my heart and my flesh cry out for the living God" (Ps. 84:1-2).

The Mount of Allegiance

Godward Climbers are Loyal to His Standard

al•le•giance—the loyalty of a subject to his/her sovereign or citizen to his/her government; fidelity, devotion. How loyal are you? The goal of this week's lessons is to challenge you to display loyalty to God in your day-to-day choices.

Base Camp

Little choices have big consequences! In this week's base camp, we'll be visiting the Great Divide to learn some lessons on loyalty. As we hike up the mountain, we'll track the steps of some people who discovered that loyalty is the path to victory.

Daily Lessons

Day 1: Covenant on the Mountain
   … Pledging the Loyalty of a Nation
Day 2: Blood on the Mountain
   … Demonstrating the Loyalty of Love
Day 3: Choice on the Mountain
   … Declaring Loyalty to a Covenant
Day 4: Instruction on the Mountain
   … Linking Loyalty to Faithfulness of the Heart
Day 5: Flag on the Mountain
   … Demonstrating Loyalty on a Daily Basis

High Points
- Mount Gerizim and Mount Ebal
- Hill of Golgotha
- Mount Carmel
- Hills of Galilee
- Hill of Rephidim

Climbing Gear
- Making the Commitment
- Staking Your Flag

Memory Pack
"Let love and faithfulness never leave you; bind them around your neck, write them on the tablet of your heart" (Prov. 3:3).

The Mount of Allegiance: Lessons on Loyalty

Exodus 17:1-15

1. A journey with God requires loyalty (17:1-4,7).

a. Are you going to _____?

b. Are you going to _____?

c. Are you going to _____?

This Base Camp
Guide will help
you follow the video
session for Summit 2.

2. Our loyalty is based on His loyalty (17:5-6).

a. He is loyal to _____.

b. He is loyal to _____.

c. He is loyal to _____.

d. He is loyal to _____.

3. Loyalty will continually be tested (17:7-8).

a. In _____.

b. In _____.

c. In _____.

4. Those who remain loyal will experience victory (17:9-15).

Hold on to His _____.

Make God your banner. Loyally align yourself with His standard. That's what it takes to conquer the Mount of Allegiance.

31

Covenant on the Mountain ...

Pledging the Loyalty of a Nation

Vertically Inclined

There once was a little dog named Hachi, who used to accompany his Japanese master to the railroad station each morning and then greet him again at the station in the evening upon his return. One day, the man died in the distant city and did not come back. That night, and every night for the next 10 years, Hachi went to the station and waited faithfully for his master—sadly trotting home again after waiting an hour. The Japanese people were so impressed by Hachi that they erected a statue of the dog on the spot where he had faithfully waited. Small replicas were sent to schools throughout the Japanese empire. Hachi became a national symbol of loyalty.

What does the word *loyalty* mean to you? Write your definition below.

_____

_____

A Covenant Demands Loyalty

The dictionary defines loyalty as being true to one's oath, obligation, or allegiance. In marriage, husband and wife take an oath to love and be faithful to one another. Being loyal to one's spouse means being true to this oath. The Bible has a special term for the oath of marriage. It's called *covenant* (Mal. 2:14). A covenant is a formal promise, agreement, or contract between two parties in which each party assumes obligation. In taking the vow of marriage, spouses enter into a "marriage covenant." Both are duty-bound to be loyal to it.

Marriage is not the only type of covenant mentioned in the Bible. Covenants were made for establishing friendships (1 Sam. 18:3), securing assistance in war (1 Kings 15:18-19), making peace (Josh. 9:15-16), promoting commerce (1 Kings 5:6-11), and selling land (Gen. 23:14-16). Not only was a covenant entered into through mutual agreement, it could also be imposed by a greater power upon a lesser one. The greater power demanded loyalty and obligated itself to protect the lesser (e.g. Josh. 9). In the Near East, it was common for the *Suzerain Kings of the Hittite Empire to unilaterally impose this type of covenant on small, surrounding states.

Most often, when the Bible uses the term covenant, it is with reference to covenants God has made. A series of divine covenants form the backbone of God's dealings with human beings.[1] In each instance, the covenant is

*A nation that controls another nation in international affairs but allows it domestic sovereignty.

32

non-negotiable. As in the Suzerain covenants, the greater power—in this case, God—defines the covenant on the lesser—humans. The book of Deuteronomy outlines the covenant God made with the Israelites.

Deuteronomy 5:6-21 outlines some specific rules that the people of Israel were to follow. Deuteronomy 28:1-14 outlines God's promise to dwell among His people and bless them. Deuteronomy 12–26 lists many more specific rules and regulations stipulated. You may want to read these passages on your own as times allows.

Read Deuteronomy 10:12-13 and 26:18-19. Fill in the chart below to summarize the covenant obligations of each party.

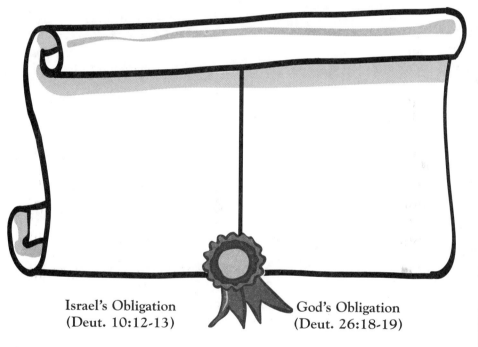

Israel's Obligation
(Deut. 10:12-13)

God's Obligation
(Deut. 26:18-19)

The Suzerain treaty was well understood by the Israelites. For years they had been in bondage to the great power, Egypt. That bondage was broken when God delivered them from Pharaoh's rule. Shortly after leaving Egypt, the people entered into a covenant with God at Mount Horeb (Sinai)—in effect, becoming God's subjects. While other small states might serve Egypt or the Hittite Empire, the Israelites owed their allegiance to God, and God alone. He was loyal to them, and expected their loyalty in return.

The Israelites reaffirmed their loyalty to the covenant at Mount Gerizim and Mount Ebal when they entered the promised land. Read today's High Point to find out more about these two mountains.

Affirming Loyalty to the Covenant (Mount Gerizim and Mount Ebal)

Mount Gerizim and Mount Ebal are 2 closely situated mountains in the central highlands of ancient Palestine, rising about 3,000 feet above the Mediterranean, roughly 40 miles north of Jerusalem. The narrow pass between the 2 mountains provides a natural amphitheater with wonderful acoustic properties. The ancient city of Shechem was located in the pass. Moses instructed the Jewish people to ceremoniously ratify their covenant with God at Gerizim and Ebal upon entering the promised land (Deut. 11:29). The location is significant as it was the place where God had appeared to their ancestor, Abraham, centuries earlier to promise the land to Abraham's descendants (Gen. 12:6).

On one of the mountains, the people were to set up great stones and inscribe them with the commandments. They were to build an altar there and offer sacrifices. Finally, Moses ordered that six tribes stand on Gerizim to pronounce blessings for obedience and the other six stand on Ebal to declare curses on disobedience (Deut. 27:9-13). The Levites (priests) were to stand in the valley between and loudly recite the stipulations of the covenant. The people were to answer "Amen" (so be it!) in response.

After conquering the center of the promised land, Joshua gathered the people at Shechem, where these ceremonies were duly performed (Josh. 8:30-35). God was granting them the land He had promised them. He was being loyal to His part of the covenant. They, in turn, recommitted themselves to be loyal to Him.

"If we look closely at this world, where God seems so utterly forgotten, we shall find that it is he, who, after all, commands the most fidelity and the most love."—Madam Anne Soymanov Swetchine[2]

Looking for Loyal Love

The covenant God made with the Israelites was presented in the format of a Suzerain treaty, but one aspect of God's covenant was very different—its motivation. Suzerain kings were motivated by the desire for power, control, fame and/or fortune. They cared very little about the individuals living in the small states.

According to Deuteronomy 7:7-9, what is unique about God's covenant? Check all that apply.

❏ It involves an insignificant group of people.
❏ It is a covenant of love.
❏ It is negotiable.
❏ It is motivated by divine affection.

God's covenant is motivated by His deep affection. It's called a "covenant of love." In contrast to earthly rulers, God had nothing to benefit by entering into a covenant with the Israelites. They couldn't offer Him anything He didn't already have. He already possessed all power, authority, honor, and riches.

There was another aspect of God's covenant that was very different. Suzerain kings demanded loyal obedience. They expected that their subjects would "toe the line" and do what the king said. The king was happy when the people simply followed the rules. God, too, wanted His people to follow the rules, but not for the sake of following the rules. God was looking for something much deeper.

In Hosea 6:4,6 in the margin, circle the words that indicate what God was really looking for.

When the Israelites obeyed the rules of the covenant—when they brought sacrifices and offerings to the temple and followed all the regulations Moses taught them—they weren't necessarily pleasing God. That's because rote obedience wasn't at the core of what God was looking for. He wanted their hearts. He wanted their loyal love. He wanted a close relationship with them. In the Hosea passage did you circle *loyalty /loyal love* and *knowledge of God*?

The Hebrew word translated "loyalty" is *chesed*. The word carries connotations of love, unity, devotion, favor, kindness, mercy, constancy, and loyalty. There is no single English word that captures all the nuances. Thus, it is translated in several ways, most often as "loving-kindness." "Knowledge" refers to intimate knowledge. It indicates a close, personal relationship. God wanted a personal relationship with His people. He was looking for loyal love.

The essence of what God was saying in His covenant with Israel was:

I love you and want to be in close relationship with you. I am God and I am holy. I cannot be in relationship with anyone who is not holy. For us to be close, you must observe the rules I give you. The rules are necessary because they make it possible for unholy people to relate to a holy God. If you don't observe them, our relationship will break down. I promise to be loyal to you. I promise to love you. I bind myself by oath to you. Give me your loyalty and love in return.

The Israelites were repeatedly unfaithful to their part of the covenant. Their hearts were not loyal to God—and they had trouble keeping all the rules. But because of God's loyal, relentless love, He instituted another covenant—a far better one. We'll learn more about the new covenant tomorrow. The bottom line is the same. God is still looking for people's hearts. He loves you. He wants your love and loyalty. Just as He longed to be close to the people of Israel, He longs to be in a close relationship with you.

"What shall I do with you, O Ephraim? What shall I do with you, O Judah? For your loyalty [loyal love] is like a morning cloud and like the dew which goes away early. ... For I delight in loyalty [loyal love] rather than sacrifice, and in the knowledge of God rather than burnt offerings" (Hos. 6:4,6, NASB®).

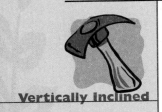

Blood on the Mountain ...
Demonstrating the Loyalty of Love

I live in the prairies of Western Canada, just east of the Rocky Mountains. Occasionally, on cloudless winter mornings, when atmospheric conditions are just right, people living here are treated to a spectacular sight—hoarfrost. Everything outdoors—every branch, twig, berry, pine needle, and slender stalk of grass—is encrusted in white, spiky crystals. The scene is particularly dazzling when the sun rises and the sparkling pristine gems are displayed against the backdrop of a cornflower-blue sky.

Hoarfrost is incredibly beautiful, but it doesn't last long. That's because it's formed by frozen dew. As soon as the sun warms the air, it disappears.

Just like morning dew, the loyalty of the nation of Israel was short-lived. Generation after generation, the people were repeatedly unfaithful to their covenant with God. God lamented, "What shall I do with you, O Ephraim? What shall I do with you, O Judah? For your loyalty [loyal love] is like a morning cloud and like the dew which goes away early" (Hos. 6:4, NASB®). God was loyal to His covenant of love, but His people were perpetually disloyal to Him. Can you imagine how God felt?

In the margin, describe how you would feel if the person you had entered into a covenant of love with were repeatedly unfaithful to you.

You probably used words like hurt, betrayed, or angry. God's covenant with Israel obviously did not bring about the lasting love relationship He desired. He anguished, "like a woman unfaithful to her husband, so you have been unfaithful to me, O house of Israel" (Jer. 3:20). One would think that after being repeatedly rejected, God would give up. But instead, He remained loyal to His people. Even more amazing, He resolved to institute a new covenant to demonstrate His faithful love toward them.

Something Old, Something New
Isaiah, Jeremiah, and Ezekiel were among those who received glimpses into what God's new covenant would entail.

Read the following three passages that speak of the new covenant:
• **Jeremiah 31:31-34** • **Ezekiel 37:26-27** • **Isaiah 59:20-21.**
Then mark whether the statements on the following page about the new covenant are true (T) or false (F).

_____ a covenant of peace that will last forever
_____ written on hearts rather than on stone tablets
_____ provides complete forgiveness of wickedness and sin
_____ makes people holy
_____ makes it possible to know God on a personal and intimate basis
_____ involves God dwelling with His people forever
_____ guarantees that relationship with God will never be broken
_____ involves the coming of a "Redeemer" and of God's Spirit
_____ provides a new list of stringent rules and regulations

The stringent rules and regulations given through Moses (called "the law") did not bring about lasting holiness (Gal. 2:16). The law was thus unable to keep people in a loyal love relationship with God. God promised a new and better covenant, one that was not based on rules and regulations. All the statements except the last one are true.

The law of the old covenant involved a system of animal sacrifices and offerings. To understand this system, you must first understand these basic facts:

- God is holy (without sin or imperfection).
- Unholy people cannot be in relationship with a holy God until they are cleansed from sin.
- God is life and the Creator of life.
- Because God is life, the natural consequence (penalty) of sin is death—separation from God.
- For an unholy person to be cleared of his or her sins and become holy, the penalty for sin (death) must be paid.

Under the old covenant, individuals were required to regularly bring animals without defect to the temple to atone for their sins. The person laid his or her hand on the head of the sacrifice symbolizing complete identification with the animal. The animal was then slaughtered and its blood sprinkled on the altar by the priests (Lev. 1:1-13). The unblemished (innocent) animal paid the price for the guilty individual by dying in place of the individual. Thus, the penalty for sin (death) was paid. The person was cleared of guilt and made holy. Individuals were to sacrifice animals for their personal sins and the priests were to sacrifice animals for the sins of the entire community. Only when the people made themselves holy in this way were they able to draw near to God (Ex. 29:42-46).

The problem with the old covenant was that people were unable to keep themselves in a state of holiness. They continually broke the rules, and there weren't enough animals in the barn to pay for all their sins. Can you imagine having to slaughter an animal every time you messed up?

The writer of Hebrews tells us that the rules of the old covenant were just a "shadow of the good things" to come (Heb. 10:1). The sacrifice of animals foreshadowed the death of Jesus Christ, God's only begotten Son, the perfect sacrifice. "We have been made holy through the sacrifice of the body of Jesus Christ once for all" (Heb. 10:10).

Read Hebrews 9:13-15. In verse 15, what is Christ called? _____

A mediator brings together parties in conflict for the purpose of reconciling them. The Bible teaches us that Jesus is the mediator of a new relationship between God and humans. Jesus brings unholy people into relationship with a holy God. According to Hebrews, it was Christ's act of dying as ransom in our place that made this possible. His blood paid for our sins and cleansed us "once for all." Never again would it be necessary to sacrifice animals.

The night before He died, Jesus called His impending death the new covenant in my blood—"poured out for many for the forgiveness of sins" (Matt. 26:28). Jesus was executed on a hill called Golgotha. Read more about this hill in today's High Point on page 39.

"Yet to all who received him, to those who believed in his name, he gave the right to become children of God" (John 1:12).

"But now a right-eousness from God, apart from law, has been made known, to which the Law and the Prophets testify. This right-eousness from God comes through faith in Jesus Christ to all who believe" (Rom. 3:21-22).

"For it is by grace you have been saved, through faith—and this not from yourselves, it is the gift of God—not by works, so that no one can boast" (Eph. 2:8-9).

Costly, Loyal Love

God promised that He would never betray His loyalty toward those He loved (Ps. 89:33). So great was His love, and so strong was His commitment, that He was willing to pay the ultimate price to make a new covenant relationship possible. "But God demonstrates his own [loyal] love for us in this: While we were still sinners, Christ died for us" (Rom. 5:8).

God's loyalty was costly. Think about what it cost God the Father and Jesus the Son to make a relationship with you possible. Pray now, thanking God for His love and sacrifices for you.

Yesterday you summarized the obligations of each party in God's covenant with Israel. God's new covenant is an offer that extends to all nations and people. If we were to itemize the new covenant obligations on a chart, God's side would be very full. He has promised us incredible things: His extravagant love, His Spirit living in us, total forgiveness, everlasting life, spiritual abundance, holiness, peace, fullness of joy, hope, security, strength, power, assurance, confidence, rest, courage, victory, a family, a home in heaven … the list goes on and on. But what are the covenant obligations on our side?

Read the verses in the margin (John. 1:12; Rom. 3:21-22; Eph. 2:8-9). Circle the words that summarize our new covenant obligation.

A Hill Worth Dying On (Hill of Golgotha)

Jesus was executed by crucifixion on the hill of Golgotha. *Golgotha* is Aramaic for "skull." The site was commonly called "the place of the skull" (Matt. 27:33; Mark 15:22; John 19:17) either because the hill physically resembled a skull, or because it was a place of execution. The Latin translation of the word skull is "calvaria," from which the name *Calvary* is derived.

The fact that the cross was visible from afar indicates that Golgotha was a hill or elevated location (Matt. 27:55). Jewish and Roman execution customs indicate that it was located outside Jerusalem's city walls, near a thoroughfare (Matt. 27:39). Apart from this, very little is known about Golgotha.

In the fourth century, Emperor Constantine built a large structure, The Church of the Holy Sepulchre, on the site then identified as Golgotha. Recent archaeological excavations place Constantine's church within Jerusalem's walls, so some scholars consider this location untenable. More recently, some have proposed that a skull-shaped rise northeast of the Damascus Gate is the true site of Golgotha.

Regardless of its location, Christ's death on the cross on Golgotha instituted the promised new covenant. Jesus knew His sacrifice would open the door for anyone to have a close, lasting relationship with God (John 3:14-16). Because of this, Golgotha was a hill worth dying on. Jesus said, "It was for this very reason I came" (John 12:27).

"The Cross is the proof that there is no length to which the love of God will refuse to go, in order to win men's hearts.—If the Cross will not waken love and wonder…nothing will."
—William Barclay[3]

You probably circled *faith*, *believe* and *receive*. The new covenant requires that we believe and receive Jesus through faith. It requires that we open our hearts and commit to a love relationship with Him. Unlike God's covenant with Israel, there are no detailed rules and regulations to follow. The new covenant does not involve a commitment to rules, but to relationship. It's because of God's grace that we are offered this free gift.

Remember the illustration of hoarfrost? It is as though God has turned the frozen dew into diamonds. Through Jesus, He has crystallized the relationship. It's now possible to have God's Holy Spirit dwell in us forever.

DAY 3

Choice on the Mountain ...

Declaring Loyalty to a Covenant

Vertically Inclined

" 'In that day,' declares the LORD, you will call me "my husband": you will no longer call me "my master." ... I will betroth you to me forever; I will betroth you in righteousness and justice, in love and compassion. I will betroth you in faithfulness and you will acknowledge the LORD" (Hos. 2:16, 19-20).

"Now it is God who makes both us and you stand firm in Christ. He anointed us, set his seal of ownership on us, and put his Spirit in our hearts as a deposit, guaranteeing what is to come" (2 Cor. 1:21-22).

The stars blinked sleepily in the black, December sky. Inside the little church, tiny, iridescent lights peeked from the boughs of plump fir trees. Candelabras cast a warm glow across the pews. Red poinsettias were placed on every available ledge. The scent of freshly cut juniper and pine accent the sense of expectancy that filled the air.

A hush had settled over the audience. I heard the creamy chiffon of my dress swish as I turned to pass the bouquet. Then, holding his hands and looking deep into his eyes, I made a covenant: "I, Mary, take you, Brent, to be my lawfully wedded husband—to have and to hold from this day forward; for better, for worse; for richer, for poorer; in sickness and in health—till death do us part." A circle of gold marked my vow of loyalty: "I give you this ring as a token and pledge of my constant faith and abiding love."

God's Sign of Loyalty

The new covenant between God and humans is similar to the covenant of love between a husband and wife. (See Hosea 2:16,19-20 in the margin. See also Ephesians 5:29-32). My husband gave me a wedding ring as a sign of his loyalty. Likewise, when we enter into the covenant relationship with God, He gives us a "token and pledge" of His loyalty.

A husband marks his loyalty to his wife with a ring. How does God mark His loyalty to us? Use 2 Corinthians 1:21-22 at left to fill in the blanks.

_____ _____ _____

As a mark of His loyalty, God anoints us, seals us, and puts a deposit in our hearts. In the Old Testament, kings, priests, and prophets were anointed with oil at the time of their induction into office (1 Sam. 9:16; Ex. 40:13-15; 1 Kings 19:16). Before the tabernacle was used, it was anointed (Ex. 40:9). Anointing was performed once, and once only, as an irrevocable sign that the person/object was chosen by God. The Greek word for *anointing* is *chrio*. It is the root of the name "Christ"—the Anointed One (Luke. 4:18).

God anoints believers with His Holy Spirit. He chooses us and sets us apart as His own. He also seals us with His Spirit (Eph. 1:13). A seal was a legal mark of ownership and/or authenticity. An individual would press His unique stamp into hot wax to give validity to legal documents or to guarantee that the contents of sacks or chests were genuine (1 Kings 21:8). The Holy Spirit is the seal of God, marking and securing every authentic believer.

Finally, the Holy Spirit is a "deposit, guaranteeing what is to come" (2 Cor. 1:22). It takes seven English words to translate the one Greek word, *arrabona*. *Arrabona* is a down payment that obligates the payer to make further payments. The word was sometimes used in reference to a ring of betrothal, which was a guarantee that the marriage would take place.[4] (In antiquity, a betrothal was just as legally binding as marriage.) God gives the Holy Spirit as a guarantee that His love relationship with us is forever and that someday we will be with Him and see Him face-to-face. The Spirit is the deposit guaranteeing that all of God's promises will be fulfilled.

The Spirit is God's pledge of eternal loyalty—the "token and pledge" of His "constant faith and abiding love." He gives the gift of the Holy Spirit to all those who choose to enter into His new covenant.

We are all painfully aware that many marriage covenants do not last. The vows of loyal love are broken. But God's loyal love is forever. His Spirit will never be taken away. His gift is irrevocable (Rom. 11:29).

Check out what the Bible says about the loyalty of God. Look up the following verses and complete the sentences.

Psalm 36:5   His faithfulness _____

Psalm 89:2   His faithfulness _____

Psalm 100:5   His faithfulness _____

Psalm 117:2   His faithfulness _____

Isaiah 25:1   His faithfulness _____

2 Timothy 2:13   His faithfulness _____

Look over the material you have studied so far this week. In the margin, summarize what you can conclude about God's loyalty toward you.

When you enter into the new covenant with God, He seals the relationship with His gift of the Holy Spirit. He permanently binds His heart to yours.

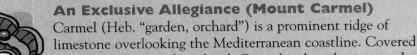

An Exclusive Allegiance (Mount Carmel)

Carmel (Heb. "garden, orchard") is a prominent ridge of limestone overlooking the Mediterranean coastline. Covered by a thick deposit of good soil, Carmel is densely vegetated with jungle, wildflowers, shrubs, and fragrant herbs. It is renowned as a symbol of beauty and splendor (Isa. 33:9, 35:2; Song of Songs 7:5). Carmel's canyon-like cliffs are dotted with caves, some of which served as ancient dwellings. The prophets Elijah and Elisha stayed there from time to time (2 Kings 2:25; 4:25).

Mount Carmel is most famous as the site of the showdown between Elijah and the prophets of Baal. Jezebel, the daughter of a foreign king, had married Israel's King Ahab to ratify an alliance between Israel and Tyre. Jezebel was a fanatical devotee of the Tyrian Baal. She had 450 of Baal's prophets and 400 prophets of the goddess Asherah on her personal staff (1 Kings 18:19). Queen Jezebel insisted that her gods have equal status with the Lord God. Her husband obliged her by constructing a pagan temple and worship sites in Israel (1 Kings 16:32).

The presence of pagan worship in the land devoted to God angered Elijah. The covenant Israel had made with God was to love and worship Him only. To draw the people back to their allegiance, Elijah challenged the pagan prophets to a showdown on Mount Carmel—a showdown that proved conclusively that the Lord was the only true God (1 Kings 18:17-40). Elijah rebuked the people of Israel for wavering in their loyalty: "How long will you waver between two opinions?" (1 Kings. 18:21).

Those who enter into a covenant of love make an exclusive choice. In marriage, we choose to forsake all other romantic love interests. A covenant with God is no different. A covenant with God requires that we choose Him and forsake all other "gods" in our lives. It is an exclusive allegiance.

"Love so amazing, so divine, demands my soul, my life, my all."
—Isaac Watts[5]

Choosing Loyalty

This week's summit is entitled The Mount of Allegiance. Up to this point, we've discussed God's allegiance (loyalty) to us. Now we turn our attention to our side of the relationship. How do we demonstrate loyalty to God?

There are two aspects to our loyalty to God. The first, and most important, is the decision to enter into a loyal, committed covenant relationship with Him. A covenant of love is an exclusive allegiance. Read today's High Point above.

What do you need to do to be part of the new covenant with God? Check all that apply.

☐ Book a church, rent a hall, and order some flowers
☐ Live up to God's standards
☐ Follow the Bible's rules and regulations
☐ Serve Jesus by ministering to other people
☐ Enter into a relationship with Jesus by accepting Him into my heart
through faith

As we learned yesterday, the new covenant does not involve a commitment to rules, but to relationship. God's gift to us is free. The only requirement is that we repent of our sins and accept Jesus into our hearts through faith, and commit to pursue a relationship with Him. We are not required to improve our behavior or live up to standards, rules, or regulations. We are not required to volunteer at the church, lead Bible studies, give money, or anything else. In the question above, the last box is the only one you should have checked.

Have you made the commitment? Close this lesson by reading today's Climbing Gear.

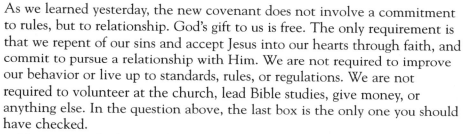

"No cord nor cable can so forcibly draw, or hold so fast, as love can do with a twined thread."
—Robert Burton[6]

Making the Commitment

Mountain climbers can talk about a climb, plan for a climb, and train for a climb, but there comes a moment when they actually have to reach out, grab hold of the rock, and take the first step. Entering into a relationship with Jesus requires that you invite Him into your heart through faith. You can pray and do that right now. You might pray something like this:

"God, I want to be in a relationship with You. I invite Jesus to come into my heart, and to forgive all my sins. I commit myself to You from this day forward—for better, for worse; for richer, for poorer; in sickness and in health—till I walk through death's door, and into your arms."

Have you committed to the new covenant relationship with God?
☐ yes   ☐ I'm not sure I can give my heart to God quite yet.

If you aren't sure about making a commitment or if you just made a commitment to God for the first time, discuss it with a leader in your small group, a church staff member, or a trusted Christian friend.

Instruction on the Mountain ...
Linking Loyalty to Faithfulness of the Heart

Vertically Inclined

"He replied, 'Isaiah was right when he prophesied about you hypocrites; as it is written: "These people honor me with their lips, but their hearts are far from me" ' "
(Mark 7:6).

A friend of mine once said, "After every wedding comes a marriage." The first aspect of loyalty to God is "tying the knot" by committing to a covenant relationship with Him. We learned about that yesterday. The second aspect of loyalty toward God is remaining true to one's covenant on a daily basis.

List some things a person can do on a daily basis to be loyal to his or her covenant of marriage.

_____

_____

_____

Did you come up with a list of specific behaviors like: "She must wash the dishes," or "He must fix the car"? I doubt it. You and I both know that loyalty to a love relationship isn't achieved by following a prescribed set of behaviors. At root, it involves faithfulness of the heart.

Heart Loyalty

The Pharisees were a group of Jews who were zealous about being loyal to the old covenant. They religiously observed all of its regulations. They read and memorized Scripture, prayed, fasted, observed the Sabbath, tithed (donated 10 percent of their food and money to the temple), offered animal sacrifices, and followed all sorts of rules for ceremonial purity (holiness). From all appearances, the Pharisees were incredibly loyal to God. But Jesus called some of them hypocrites. He did not think they were loyal at all.

According to Mark 7:6 (in the margin), what was the Pharisees' problem?

_____

Jesus knew that seemingly loyal outward behavior does not always indicate inward loyalty of the heart. It's the same way in any love relationship. Just because a spouse is physically faithful doesn't mean that his or her heart is true.

In His Sermon on the Mount, Jesus taught that true loyalty involves much more than outward behavior. According to Jesus, it's hypocritical to think we are being loyal to God's command, "do not murder," if we slander and hate (Matt 5:21-22). It's hypocritical to think we are being loyal to God's command, "do not commit adultery," if our hearts are filled with lust (Matt. 5:27-28). It's hypocritical to profess friendship with God while refusing to be friends with a brother (Matt. 5:23-24). It's hypocritical to love only those whom we regard as deserving of our love (Matt. 5:43-45). Find out more about the Sermon on the Mount by reading today's High Point.

"Wicked men obey from fear, good men, from love."—Aristotle[7]

👀 Taking Loyalty to a New Level (Hills of Galilee)

Palestine was divided into three provinces: Judea, Samaria, and Galilee. Galilee—the largest and most northern province—was some 60 by 33 miles in area. Galilee (Heb., *Gaul*, meaning "circle") was encircled with several lines of hills separated by broad, fertile valleys. Watered by numerous springs and winter rains, the hills of Galilee were ideal for farming. The countryside flourished with vineyards, olive orchards, and herds of sheep and goats.

Galilee was renowned for its cultural diversity. Travel and trade routes traversed the province in all directions. Because of the abundance of fish, the Sea of Galilee attracted a larger and more varied population than anywhere else in Palestine. This prosperous district had links with all parts of the known world—hence the name "Galilee of the nations" (Isa. 9:1, KJV).

The province of Galilee was the scene of the early ministry of Jesus. He lived in Nazareth (Matt. 21:11), performed His first miracle at Cana (John 2:1), and called His first disciples at Capernaum (Matt. 4:18-21). It was near Capernaum that He "went up on a mountainside" to deliver the message known as the Sermon on the Mount (Matt. 5–7). Though the exact location is unknown, several hills in the area functioned as natural amphitheaters and could have been used for that purpose.

Some scholars have called the mountain where Jesus spoke "the Sinai of the New Testament."[8] It was at Mount Sinai that Moses taught the Israelites how to be loyal to the old covenant. In the same fashion, Jesus ascended the side of a mountain to teach His followers how to be loyal to the impending new covenant. In the Sermon on the Mount, Jesus took loyalty to a new level. He taught that loyalty went far beyond external standards of behavior. True loyalty begins with faithfulness of the heart.

45

Jesus' standard for loyalty is radical. He calls for a deep loyalty of the heart far beyond rote obedience. It's a loyalty that flows from the inside out—from a heart that is head-over-heels in love with God. It's the type of loyalty that cannot be achieved through external rules or human effort. It can only be achieved through God's Spirit. That's why the new covenant is so much better than the old. The Holy Spirit, who lives in us, puts God's commands in our hearts and writes them on our minds (Heb. 10:16). We are both perfect and being made perfect (holy). Thus, our loyalty to God is both an accomplished fact (Heb.10:10) and an ongoing process (Heb. 10:14).

The Holy Spirit is our internal compass to teach and guide us in God's ways. The Spirit implants God's commands in our hearts. He also gives us the desire and power to remain loyal to God on a daily basis by doing what God wants.

Read 2 Timothy 1:7 in the margin. Identify the three things God, through His Spirit, has given you.

1. _____ 2. _____ 3. _____

How do power, love, and self-discipline help us demonstrate loyalty to God on a daily basis? Look up and read each reference in your Bible and match them to the summary statements that follow.

A. Titus 2:11-15   B. John 14:23-24   C. 1 John 5:3   D. Luke 6:46-49

_____ Those who love Jesus obey His teaching and experience His (and His Father's) intimate presence.

_____ A rock-solid love relationship with Christ is built on the foundation of hearing His words and putting them into practice.

_____ God's grace teaches us to say "no" to sin and "yes" to self-controlled, upright, godly living.

_____ Those who love God delight in obedience. God's commands are not burdensome to them. They are eager to do what He says.

Reread Luke 6:46-48.
In the frame, write or draw an illustration of how to build a rock-solid loyal love relationship with God.

"For God did not give us a spirit of timidity, but a spirit of power, of love and of self-discipline" (2 Tim. 1:7).

A couple of years ago, I was leaving home for an overnight conference. Just before I left, I quickly took a load of laundry out of the dryer and piled it Everest-like in the middle of the family room. I asked my son to fold the laundry so it wouldn't get wrinkled. When I returned, I found that he had swept the kitchen, vacuumed the living room, and placed fresh flowers on the table to welcome me home. I was thrilled ... until I saw the mountain of laundry, untouched and unfolded. My son had done all sorts of things to please me, but had not done the one and only thing I had asked of him.

Even though my son had done so much to please me, I remember feeling disappointed and annoyed. Upon reflection, I realized that his behavior is not unlike my own. I do many things to express my devotion to God. But am I careful to listen and do the one thing He asks of me?

Ask the Lord what "one thing" He wants you to do today to demonstrate your loyalty to Him. Mend a relationship? Encourage someone? Change a speech habit? Set aside some time to read the Bible or pray? Write it below.

"Love is what loyalty is all about."—M. Kassian

_____

_____

We demonstrate our loyal love for God by obeying Him and doing what pleases Him (1 John 3:22). We do not obey because of duty, but because we are motivated and empowered by the Spirit He has deposited in our hearts. The obedience springs from love, not obligation. It's like the difference between a man bringing his wife flowers to appease her nagging, and bringing her flowers because he delights in her. The action is the same, but the motivation is completely different. Love is what loyalty is all about.

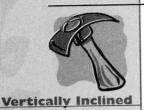

Vertically Inclined

Flag on the Mountain...

Demonstrating Loyalty on a Daily Basis

All over the world, flags are used as symbols to identify a country's land, its government, its people, and its ideals. This has been the case throughout history. The early Israelites marched and camped under four large, beautifully embroidered and ornamented flags—designating their position north, south, east, and west of the tabernacle (Num. 2:2-3,10,18,25). Individual tribes bore smaller banners of identification.

Flags, banners, and coats of arms are also called "standards." That's because they call for loyalty or devotion to a person, group, and/or set of values. Every morning in the United States, school children stand, right hand over their heart, to pledge allegiance to their "standard." They vow to be loyal to their republic, "one nation, under God, indivisible, with liberty and justice for all."

Standards are rallying points. Whenever a flag or banner is raised, it's meant to rally those who are loyal to it. That's why flags were so important in battles. The flag led the charge. Those who were loyal followed. If the soldier who was carrying the flag was killed or wounded, others would "rally around the flag" to prevent the enemy from capturing it. Fighting for and protecting the flag was of paramount importance, for the flag represented the value for which the soldiers fought.

God has lifted His banner. He beckons all people to come and loyally align themselves with His standard: "See, I will beckon to the Gentiles, I will lift up my banner to the peoples" (Isa. 49:22).

Read Isaiah 11:10; Acts 13:21-23; and Song of Songs 2:4.
On the flag at right, draw symbols to represent the Banner of God.

In Exodus 17:15 (KJV), Moses called God "Jehovah-nissi." What is the translation of this name of

God?_____

Learn more about why Moses used this name for God in today's High Point.

The Upheld Standard (Hill of Rephidim)

They didn't see it coming ... A tribe of fierce, rapacious nomads attacked them from behind. A few days prior, Moses had nicknamed the place *Meribah*—"testing"—because there, the Israelites had questioned the loyalty of God. God proved Himself faithful. With one blow from the staff of God, water gushed from the rock and defeated their thirst. Now, the Israelites faced an even more formidable enemy: the Amalekites.

This time there was no grumbling and questioning. The Israelites listened as Moses laid out the plan: He would climb to the top of Rephidim and hold up the staff. Joshua would lead the charge in the valley below. The next day they put the plan into action. But when Moses got tired and lowered the staff, the Amalekites started to win. Propped up on a rock, with two friends lending strength to his extended arms, Moses managed to hold the standard high. Ultimately, it was the upheld standard, not the skill of the warriors, that secured the victory. That's why, after the battle was over, Moses worshiped God as "Jehovah-nissi"—"God is my Banner" (Ex. 17:8-15, *The Message*).

Holding up God's standard brings victory. As the psalmist said, "We will shout for joy when you are victorious and will lift up our banners in the name of our God ... Some trust in chariots and some in horses, but we trust in the name of the Lord our God" (Ps. 20:5,7).

"Faith of our fathers, holy faith—
We will be true to thee till death."
—Frederick William Faber[9]

Loyal in Little Things

Are you loyal to God? Are you faithful in little things? This week, on the Mount of Allegiance, we learned a lot about loyalty. God isn't looking for people who are focused on following rules, constantly worried about the "dos and don'ts" of the Christian life. He's looking for loyalty of the heart.

Heart loyalty takes obedience to a much higher level than adhering to a set of rules ever could. We obey because we want to, not because we have to. As Jesus said, "If you love me, you will obey what I command" (John 14:23). The gift of God's indwelling Spirit sets us free from the rule of sin and death and inclines our hearts towards righteousness. As friends of Jesus, we are free to be loyal to Him by consistently choosing to do what is right.

See how loyal you really are. Take the "Test of Loyalty" on pages 50-51. After each command, mark an X on the scale to indicate how loyal you are to Jesus in obeying that command.

Test of Loyalty

1. Do all things without grumbling or complaining (Phil. 2:4).

I am disloyal. **I am loyal.**

2. "Be patient, bearing with one another in love" (Eph. 4:2).

I am disloyal. **I am loyal.**

3. Study and correctly handle the word of truth [the Bible] (2 Tim. 2:15).

I am disloyal. **I am loyal.**

4. "Love one another deeply from the heart" (1 Pet. 1:22).

I am disloyal. **I am loyal.**

5. Think about things that are true, pure, right, lovely, and praiseworthy (Phil. 2:11).

I am disloyal. **I am loyal.**

6. "Rid yourselves of all malice, and all deceit, hypocrisy, envy, and slander" (1 Pet. 2:1).

I am disloyal. **I am loyal.**

7. "Do not love the world or anything in the world" (1 John 2:15).

I am disloyal. **I am loyal.**

8. Do "not give up meeting together" [for worship] (Heb. 10:25).

I am disloyal. **I am loyal.**

9. "Be completely humble and gentle" (Eph. 4:2).

I am disloyal. **I am loyal.**

10. "Be holy in all you do" (1 Pet. 1:15).

I am disloyal. **I am loyal.**

11. Do not even tolerate a hint of sexual immorality (Eph. 5:3).

I am disloyal. **I am loyal.**

12. "Pray … on all occasions" (Eph. 5:18).

I am disloyal. **I am loyal.**

13. "Show proper respect to everyone" (1 Pet. 2:17).

I am disloyal. **I am loyal.**

14. "Get rid of all bitterness, rage, and anger." Forgive (Eph. 4:31-32).

I am disloyal.   I am loyal.

15. Do not be insensitive to sensuality, impurity, and other evil (Eph. 4:18-19).

I am disloyal.   I am loyal.

16. Give cheerfully (2 Cor. 9:6-8).

I am disloyal.   I am loyal.

17. "Do not repay evil with evil or insult with insult, but with blessing" (1 Pet. 3:9).

I am disloyal.   I am loyal.

18. "Have nothing to do with the fruitless deeds of darkness" (Eph. 5:11).

I am disloyal.   I am loyal.

19. "Do not be anxious about anything" (Phil. 4:6).

I am disloyal.   I am loyal.

20. "Be imitators of God" (Eph. 5:1).

I am disloyal.   I am loyal.

Circle three areas in which you need to work on being more loyal.

Gear up with today's Climbing Gear. Find out how to "Stake Your Flag" on the right side of the divide.

"A little thing is a little thing, but faithfulness in a little thing becomes a great thing."—Plato[10]

Staking Your Flag

Think about the last show you watched, the last music you listened to, the last magazine or book you read, how you behaved in a significant relationship. Were you loyal to Jesus? Ask Him. Jot your thoughts in the margin if He convicts you about anything.

Every day you make hundreds of choices. With each one, you have the opportunity to make God your banner or stake your flag on the other side of the divide. A small difference in position can make a world of difference! The next time you have a choice to make, ask Jesus: "To be loyal, where do I stake my flag?" Choose God's side in order to grow in loyal love.

The Mount of Appraisal
Godward Climbers Evaluate and Make Adjustments

ap•prais•al—to size up and estimate the value of under the direction of a competent authority. To carefully evaluate; to gauge or assess. Are you in the habit of carefully appraising your position? The goal this week is to challenge you to evaluate and make adjustments on an ongoing basis.

Base Camp
There are dangers in high places! David "Stargazer" Thompson managed to map his way through the mountain pass by evaluating his position in relation to a fixed point. In this week's Base Camp you'll see that the way to make it through high places is to keep yourself aligned with the humble heart of Christ.

Daily Lessons
Day 1: Into Thin Air
    … Danger in High Places
Day 2: Head in the Clouds
    … Building High Places
Day 3: Mountain Madness
    … Falling from High Places
Day 4: Fear of Heights
    … Avoiding High Places
Day 5: Before a Fall
    … The Way Through High Places

High Points
- High Places (Bamah)
- "Mount" Babylon
- Kingdom Mount
- The Destroying Mount
- The Stones of Gilgal

Climbing Gear
- American Idol
- Sawdust and Planks

Memory Pack
"All of you, clothe yourselves with humility toward one another, because 'God opposes the proud but gives grace to the humble.' Humble yourselves, therefore, under God's mighty hand, that he may lift you up in due time" (1 Pet. 5:5-6).

The Mount of Appraisal: Passing Through High Places
Luke 18:9-14

Summit 3—

The Mount of Appraisal

This Base Camp Guide will help you follow the video session for Summit 3.

1. Check Your Altitude: _____ versus _____.

- "High Places" represent _____ and _____.

- *Do you claim the high place as your own?*

2. Check Your Focus: _____ versus _____.

- Pride can hide under a _____ _____.

- *Are you more concerned about what people see or what God sees?*

3. Check Your Orientation: _____ versus _____.

- Prides weighs personal _____.

- *Are you self-sufficient, or do you consistently rely on God?*

4. Check Your Point of Reference: _____ verses

_____.

- Pride _____.

- *Do you view yourself in light of other people or gaze at the Star?*

Are you finding your way through high places? Humbly evaluate and make adjustments. Work at becoming a "Star Gazer." That's the way to conquer the Mount of Appraisal.

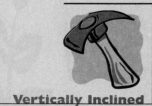

Vertically Inclined

Into Thin Air ...
Danger in High Places

Death Zone. That's the name of the region on Everest above 25,000 feet where the risk of dying is most extreme. Extreme freezing temperatures present the danger of frostbite and hypothermia. But the biggest danger would exist even if the top of the mountain were as warm and balmy as the Caribbean: high altitude illness.

At high altitudes, the air is thin. Therefore, each breath contains less oxygen. Without adequate oxygen, the body becomes critically ill. Experts say that an individual taken from sea level and unceremoniously dropped on top of Everest would lose consciousness and die within a matter of minutes. The body can acclimate somewhat if the ascent is made carefully and slowly, but even so, no one can survive for long in such a high place.

The shortage of oxygen at high altitudes causes a variety of illnesses. Acute Mountain Sickness (AMS) is characterized by shortness of breath, exhaustion, vomiting, headache, and decreased balance and coordination. High Altitude Cerebral Edema (HACE) and High Altitude Pulmonary Edema (HAPE) are severe, life-threatening conditions that involve swelling of the brain and the lungs. But the most profound and common effect of being in the death zone is mental disorientation. Because the brain requires more oxygen than the rest of the body, one's mental condition deteriorates faster than one's physical condition. Bluntly stated: At extremely high altitudes, people get stupid quick.

The Bible talks about the danger of high places. But the high altitude illness it's concerned with is a spiritual, rather than physical, condition. Scripture speaks of many who have been afflicted with this critical illness.

Read 2 Kings 17:9-12. The Israelites were demonstrating symptoms of spiritual high altitude illness. List their symptoms.

To find out more about high places, read today's High Point.

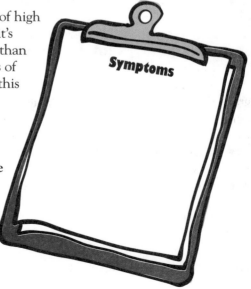

Symptoms

Hills, Stones, Trees and Groves: High Places (Bamah)

High places are extremely significant. A high place is the part of the landscape that's the most prominent. It's the focal point—like the throne in a throne room. Thus, high places are closely associated with the concept of "lordship." Metaphorically, they symbolize dominance and control: He who controls the heights controls the land.

The Hebrew word for *high place* (*bamah*: "to be high") is used over 100 times in the Old Testament. Ancient peoples used high places as sites on which to honor their gods. Hilltops were planted with beautiful groves of trees, furnished with sacred stones, altars, wooden pillars or poles, and ornamented with elaborate tapestries (1 Kings 14:23; Ezek. 16:16). In some cases, a building called a "house of high places," was constructed there (1 Kings 12:31, KJV).

People went to high places to burn incense and offer sacrifices to the gods (1 Kings 22:43). Furthermore, the sites served as the locale for social gatherings, feasts, and festivals (1 Kings 12:32), which involved dancing and revelry, as well as adultery and prostitution (1 Kings 14:24; Amos 2:8; Ezek. 22:9). Because of their garden-like beauty, high places were also used as places of rest and retreat (1 Sam. 22:6).

In Israel's history, the two idols most often associated with high places were Asherah and Baal. Asherah (meaning "grove") was the female Canaanite goddess of fertility, sexuality, love, and war who held forth the promise of fortune and happiness. Asherah was sometimes called "Queen of Heaven," and was also referred to by other names such as Ashtoreth, Astarte, Venus, and Istar. Asherah was the consort and lover of Baal, a nature deity, or god of the weather. The Hebrew noun *ba'al* means "master," "owner," or "possessor." This god was the male god of fertility—an erotic, prodigious lover and giver of abundance.

Establishing and visiting high places was a common cultural practice. People took part in the ritual in hope that the deities would supernaturally grant them love, prosperity, success, and fulfillment. The Israelites were commanded to lay bare the high places and demolish all idols when they took possession of the promised land (Num. 33:52). God alone was the "most high God" (Gen. 14:22). He was to be their focal point. He was the One who was to occupy the "high place" of their lives.

"Such arrogance, I believe, is dangerous for any climber."
—Jon Krakauer[1]

You may think that high places and idols are a thing of the past. But I believe that the concepts are just as significant today as they were thousands of years ago. Each one of us needs to continually examine the "high place" of our heart to see if any "idols" have taken up residence.

Based on the information you read in today's High Point, see if you can come up with a contemporary definition for the following terms. Write your definitions on the lines provided.

High Place: _____

_____

Idol: _____

_____

Here are my definitions: A *high place* is like the throne in the throne room of my life. It's my focal point. It's the "front and center" prominent position I give to that which is most important to me.

An idol is anything I put in a high place that should not be there. Any person, thing, value, or desire that takes a front and center, over-and-above-God position in my life can be called an idol.

And speaking of *idols* … check out today's Climbing Gear on page 57 to see if you can identify some modern-day American idols.

List some modern-day idols below.

_____

Can you identify any idols in your own heart? ❑ yes ❑ no ❑ I'm not sure. If yes, list them here.

_____

_____

Danger Zone

As we learned at the beginning of today's lesson, one of the most profound dangers of being in the death zone is mental disorientation. In the spiritual realm the situation is similar. A person's mindset can be dangerously affected in high places.

American Idol

Have you ever looked for an American idol? I'm not talking about auditioning for a TV show. And I'm not talking about those weird-looking, multi-armed stone or wood statues with one eye like a Cyclops—the ones you've seen assuming twisted, bizarre poses in books or in museums of ancient history. I'm talking about real, modern-day idols: idols that we can spot all around us—perhaps even in our own lives. People in modern-day America have just as many idols as the people in the Ancient Mid-East did. And we don't have to climb to the top of a hill or mountain to spot them.

Can you identify some modern-day idols? Here's a hint … one of the biggest and most obvious of these idols lives in people's wallets. Money is a huge idol. Can you think of some other modern-day idols? Along with the biggies, try to identify some smaller, less conspicuous ones. Remember, an *idol* is any person, thing, value, or desire that takes a front-and-center, over-and-above-God position in your life.

"Humility is the key to being a good alpinist." —Barry Blanchard[2]

Read Isaiah 2:11-18. According to verses 17 and 18, what mindset is characteristic of those who have idols in high places?

What mindset is necessary in order for idols to totally disappear?

Those who have anything other than God as the focal point of their lives are filled with pride. Pride is one of the biggest dangers Godward climbers face. This week, on the Mount of Appraisal, we'll learn how to humbly evaluate and make adjustments so we don't get caught in this spiritual death zone. Close today's lesson by asking God to show you if you have idols in high places. Ask Him to help you demolish them.

Head in the Clouds ...
Building High Places

The mound of snow on the playground was perfect for the game. At the red-bricked grade school I attended, this particular game was a favorite at recess time. When the bell rang, the first boy or girl to make it to the top got to be "king." The other children gathered at the base of the pile, waiting a turn to challenge the king's position. One by one, they'd storm up the hill and wrestle its occupant. After a short scuffle, one child would prevail and the other would come tumbling down—arms and legs flailing—mitts, hat, and scarf covered in clumps of frosty white crystals. With raised arms, the child who managed to stay on top would then exercise his or her bragging rights: "I'm the king of the castle, and you're the dirty rascal! NAH-nah-nah-NAH-nah!" he or she would taunt.

A King-of-the-Castle Legacy

"King of the Castle" is a silly, childish game, but unfortunately it's a game that's played in the lives of most adults—albeit on a much more sophisticated level. In the grown-up game there are no physical hills, but still, people fight with one another for superiority. Everyone wants to be "King of the Castle." Emotionally and psychologically we knock one another down so we can claim the high place as our own.

"It is an amiable illusion, which the shape of our planet prompts, that every man is at the top of the world." —Ralph Waldo Emerson[3]

Wanting to be "King of the Castle" is nothing new. In antiquity, one of the first persons to go on record as playing the King of the Castle game was Nimrod, the great-grandson of Noah, the founder of the city of Babylon and a builder of the tower of Babel (Gen. 10:8,10). Nimrod's King of the Castle legacy was carried on for centuries by his descendants and by the inhabitants of Babylon. Spiritually, all those who arrogantly build high places participate in this legacy.

Read the following verses describing the history of the people of Babylon.
- "Come, let us build ourselves a city, with a tower that reaches to the heavens, so that we may make a name for ourselves" (Gen. 11:4).
- "Babylon, the jewel of kingdoms, the glory of the Babylonians' pride" (Isa. 13:19).
- "Babylon the Great" (Rev. 16:19).
- "Ruthless and impetuous people, who sweep across the whole earth to seize dwelling places not their own" (Hab. 1:6).

- "They are a law to themselves and promote their own honor" (Hab. 1:7).
- "[Their] own strength is their god" (Hab. 1:11).
- They say, "I will ascend to heaven; I will raise my throne above the stars of God … I will ascend above the tops of the clouds; I will make myself like the Most High" (Isa. 14:13-14).

In Jeremiah 50:31, God calls Babylon the "arrogant one." Use the verses above to complete the following puzzle.*

- Where the people lived (Isa. 13:19)
- What they were filled with (Isa. 13:19)
- What they wanted to do for themselves (Hab. 1:7)
- What they wanted to receive (Hab. 1:7)
- How they wanted to be regarded (Rev. 16:19)
- What they wanted to make for themselves (Gen. 11:4)
- Whose strength they depended on (Hab. 1:11)
- What they wanted to raise up for themselves (Isa. 14:13-14)

Building High Towers

Some scholars believe Nimrod, the great-grandson of Noah, was the founder of the city of Babel. The city of Babel may later have grown into the city of Babylon. Babylon was founded on an arid plain situated beside the Euphrates River, 56 miles south of modern-day Baghdad, Iraq—a place Scripture calls the "Desert by the Sea" (Isa. 21:1). Nimrod's clan had been commanded by God to disperse throughout the land of Canaan. Instead, they decided to settle on the plain and build a monumental city "with a tower that reaches to the heavens, so that we may make a name for ourselves" (Gen. 11:4).

High towers were common during that era. Sumerian city-states, located in the land south of Babylon, were temple communities controlled by a class of priest-bureaucrats in the name of the local god. The central feature of each city was a terraced, tower-like temple with steps leading to its summit, called a *ziggurat*—a word derived from the Assyrian *zigguratu*, meaning "high." Nimrod and his clan intended to build a ziggurat higher and grander than any the Sumerians had built.

---

* ANSWERS: Babylon, Pride, Promote, Honor, Great, Name, Own, Throne

The name of Nimrod's city, Babylon, was derived from the name of the tower, Babel, which is a play on words of the Hebrew verb meaning "to confuse" and the Assyrian word meaning "gate of the gods." It was at Babel that God countered the prideful arrogance of humanity by "confusing" its language. But this didn't put an end to the prideful legacy started by Nimrod. Hundreds of years later, in the 18th century B.C., King Hammurabi consolidated his empire by establishing a central government in Babylon. Babylon became the center of power and control for the entire region. Consequently, the empire came to be known as the "Babylonian Empire."

Hammurabi improved Babylon's irrigation, agriculture, and transport system, and constructed many temples and buildings. But it wasn't until the time of King Nebuchadnezzar II (625-539 B.C.) that the city reached mountain-like proportions. Find out more about the towering city-mountain of Babylon by reading today's High Point on page 61.

Isaiah 47:7-10 records the prideful arrogance of the Babylonians. Read this passage in your Bible and complete the chart by identifying the word or phrase from each verse that illustrates the prideful attitude listed on the left. The first one is done for you.

Attitude	Verse	Word or phrase that illustrates this prideful attitude
Self-assured	v. 7	"I will continue forever."
Self-enamored	v. 7	
Self-indulgent	v. 8	
Self-absorbed	v. 8	
Self-secure	v. 8	
Self-reliant	v. 9	
Self-satisfied	v. 10	
Self-governed	v. 10	
Self-centered	v. 10	

Yesterday we learned that an idol is any person, thing, value, or desire that takes a front-and-center, over-and-above-God position in an individual's life. The Babylonians worshiped many man-made idols like Marduk, Ishtar, and Baal. But their biggest idol was the "god" they saw in their own mirrors—the idol, "Me."

Do you "self-idolize"? Look over the attitudes listed on the left side of the chart you completed. Do you struggle with any of these attitudes? Circle the attitudes with which you struggle.

The Towering City Mountain: "Mount" Babylon

Under the rule of Nebuchadnezzar, Babylon became a city of mountain-like proportions. Some authorities estimate it boasted 20 million inhabitants. It was the largest, most spectacular city of the ancient world.

The ancient historian Herodotus reports that the outer walls of Babylon were 56 miles in length, 80 feet thick, and 320 feet high (That's more than a football field in height). The city terraced upward, mountain-like from this imposing cliff-like perimeter. Architects designed beautiful stone arches to beautify the city, and a system to channel water from the Euphrates into a series of cool streams, pools, and cascading waterfalls. The "Hanging Gardens," one of the 7 wonders of the ancient world, graced the terrace steps with palms, exotic flowers, and lush green foliage.

Nebuchadnezzar built a magnificent shrine to his city god, Marduk, in the middle of Babylon. The 7-storied ziggurat, soaring 300 feet high, was likely built on the site of the original Tower of Babel. It was embellished with alabaster, lapis lazuli, and precious stones. Its walls were coated in solid gold. Archaeologists estimate that the main room of the temple contained more than 18 tons of the sparkling precious metal. A processional street, arched at its opening by the elaborately enameled Ishtar gate, connected the temple to the inner city.

Babylon was like a green, bejeweled mountain in the midst of a dry, desert plain. It was a city of incredible beauty, wealth, and power—the "jewel of kingdoms" (Isa 13:19). Travelers were overwhelmed by its magnificence and opulence. But according to the Bible, the city had one major flaw, its rulers and people were arrogant (Jer. 50:31). They took pride in themselves and in their idols and refused to acknowledge Yahweh, the Most High God.

"If anyone would like to acquire humility, I can, I think, tell him the first step. The first step is to realize that one is proud. And a biggish step too." —C.S. Lewis[4]

The first step in dealing with pride is coming before God and humbly admitting that it is present in our hearts. Take some time to do that now.

Mountain Madness ...
Falling from High Places

He breathed in the soft, cool evening air and sighed with contentment. The seclusion of the rooftop garden always soothed him. There would be no headaches or bad dreams tonight. Picking a pomegranate from an overhanging branch and absentmindedly rubbing it between his palms, the king began a leisurely stroll around the perimeter. The view was panoramic. This was the ideal place from which to admire the vast splendor of his magnificent city.

The last muted rays of the fading sun settled on the walls of the temple, sending amber leaves of light dancing over the surface of the still water. On the far side, a narrow ribbon of water spilled over the stone and slowly gurgled its way down to the garden below. The sweet fragrance of narcissus laced the air. The king inhaled deeply, and for a moment closed his eyes. "It's beautiful," he noted with satisfaction, "the most beautiful place on earth!"

In two great strides, he bounded up the steps to the highest vantage point. Here the view was unrestricted. Laughing, he tossed the pomegranate over the edge and listened to it splat on the glazed ceramic brick below. Extending his arms in child-like exuberance, he pivoted full circle—eyes feasting on the landscape. "Awesome! Absolutely amazing!" No one on earth had ever built such a spectacular city!

"Ha!" All the stresses of the day were gone. The king could feel the energy flowing back into his veins. He was alone, and feeling quite uninhibited. He laughed again and jumped up on the thick stone rail. "Hey, World!" he shouted. "Take a look at me!" No answer.

"If only those fat, stodgy royal advisors could see me now," he chortled. With a great flourish and a toss of his head, the king continued his theatrics. Cupping his mouth, he bellowed at the top of his lungs, "Is not this the great Babylon I have built as the royal residence, by my mighty power and for the glory of my majesty?"

The loud reply from above startled him. In an instant, he remembered the dream, and his heart was gripped with fear.

The book of Daniel contains portions of King Nebuchadnezzar's personal diary. Read his account of the dream in Daniel 4:4-18. Illustrate the three parts of the dream in the three frames on the top of page 63.

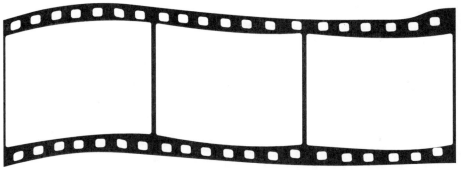

| 1. The large, strong tree | 2. Cut down | 3. Living with wild animals |

Daniel, an exiled Jew and one of the King's spiritual advisors, interpreted the dream for Nebuchadnezzar. Read about Nebuchadnezzar's other dream, "the mountain that filled the earth," in today's High Point.

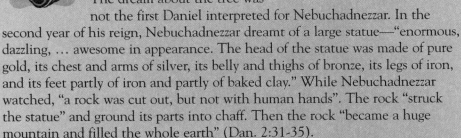

"He that is proud eats up himself; pride is his own glass, his own trumpet, his own chronicle!"— Shakespeare, *Troilus and Cressida* [5]

The Mountain that Fills the Earth: Kingdom Mount

The dream about the tree was not the first Daniel interpreted for Nebuchadnezzar. In the second year of his reign, Nebuchadnezzar dreamt of a large statue—"enormous, dazzling, ... awesome in appearance. The head of the statue was made of pure gold, its chest and arms of silver, its belly and thighs of bronze, its legs of iron, and its feet partly of iron and partly of baked clay." While Nebuchadnezzar watched, "a rock was cut out, but not with human hands". The rock "struck the statue" and ground its parts into chaff. Then the rock "became a huge mountain and filled the whole earth" (Dan. 2:31-35).

Daniel explained that the dream was a vision of things to come. The gold head represented Nebuchadnezzar's Babylonian kingdom. The other materials represented the lesser kingdoms that would subsequently dominate the Middle East (the empires of Medo-Persia, Greece, and Rome). Following this, Daniel reported, the God of heaven will "set up a kingdom which shall never be destroyed and the kingdom shall ... break in pieces and consume all these kingdoms, and it shall stand forever" (Dan. 2:44, KJV).

The rock in Nebuchadnezzar's dream represents the kingdom of Jesus Christ. The point of the dream was to teach Nebuchadnezzar about the greatness of God. Comparing the power and authority of God's rule to that of earthly kingdoms is like comparing a massive mountain to a handful of chaff. God is above all power and rule and authority. Christ's kingdom is the "mountain that fills the earth."

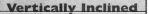

Pride Comes Before a Fall

The dream about the statue illustrated that Nebuchadnezzar's great dynasty was nothing in comparison to the kingdom of God. Daniel explained that the dream about the tree was meant to warn Nebuchadnezzar about the impending consequences of his prideful, domineering spirit. The tree represented King Nebuchadnezzar whose kingdom had become great and strong. Daniel warned that if Nebuchadnezzar didn't repent of his prideful attitude and behavior, God would strike him down: "You will be driven away from people and will live with the wild animals; you will eat grass like cattle and be drenched with the dew of heaven" (Dan. 4:25). The dream came true just twelve months later. One night, on the rooftop of his palace, Nebuchadnezzar was struck with lycanthropy.

Lycanthropy is a mental psychosis in which the patient has delusions of being a wild animal. The patient exhibits behavior such as growling, scratching and clawing, snarling, gnawing and animalistic aggression. Under God's judgment, the proud and dignified monarch instantly became a raving maniac. The condition lasted for seven years until Nebuchadnezzar "raised [his] eyes toward heaven and [his] sanity was restored" (Dan. 4:34).

Read Daniel 4:25-27, 34-37. Summarize what God wanted Nebuchadnezzar to learn.

_____

_____

Nebuchadnezzar learned to avoid "looking down" at others by "looking up" at God. Unfortunately, his successor, King Belteshazzar, didn't learn the same lesson (Dan. 5). In the end, God judged Belteshazzar, the city of Babylon, and the entire Babylonian empire for their prideful spirits. Read more about Babylon's destroying Mountain of Pride in the High Point on page 65.

How about you? Do you compare yourself to others to try and determine your self-worth? Or do you keep your eyes fixed on God? On the scale below, circle the number that corresponds to your attitude.

◀ 0   1   2   3   4   5   6   7   8   9   10 ▶

I look around at
others. (Pride)

I look up at God.
(Humility)

Killer Heights (The Destroying Mount)

One of the names of the city of Babylon is "destroying mountain" (Jer. 51:25). Babylon's massive walled perimeter, terraced streets, and towering ziggurat gave the city a mountain-like appearance. It was also "higher" than all other cities in terms of its power and eminence. Thus, though it was built on a plain and not on the heights, Babylon is called a mountain.

This mountain-like city was called a destroying mountain for several reasons. To begin, the Babylonians were notoriously violent when conquering and subduing surrounding nations. Their thirst for power caused them to cruelly oppress and destroy those whom they conquered. Furthermore, Scripture accuses Babylon of destroying the whole earth by poisoning it with a thirst for riches and power, and with an attitude of prideful arrogance. Babylon "made the whole earth drunk. The nations drank her wine; therefore they have now gone mad" (Jer. 51:7). The pride of Babylon enticed others to go mad with pride. In the book of Revelation, Babylon symbolizes the ungodly power of the end times (14:8; 16:19; 17:5; 18:2,10,21). Revelation depicts it as the great whore—the mother of harlots and the abomination of the earth (17:1,5; 19:2).

Babylon illustrates the epitome of self-centeredness, self-indulgence, self-reliance, and self-exaltation. In a word, Babylon embodies pride: the attitude that exalts self, rejects God, and seeks to dominate and control others. It's a killer height that destroys individuals, families, communities, and nations.

In Daniel 4:4, Nebuchadnezzar described himself as "[self] contented" and "prosperous." He gleaned his sense of self by comparing himself to others. After his illness, Nebuchadnezzar's attitude changed drastically. Instead of looking at others to evaluate his self-worth, Nebuchadnezzar humbly kept his eyes fixed on God. Prior to his illness, Nebuchadnezzar would have rated about a "1" on the scale of pride below. After his illness, he would rate on the higher end of the scale.

> "A proud man is always looking down on things and people; and, of course, as long as you're looking down, you can't see something that's above you." —C.S. Lewis [6]

I'm filled with pride whenever I have the mindset that "it's all about me" rather than humbly acknowledging that it's all about God. Close today's lesson by praying and asking the Holy Spirit to reveal the pride of your heart to you. Over the next few days, evaluate your attitude on an ongoing basis. Watch to determine if your actions are motivated by pride ("It's all about me!") or humility ("It's all about God!").

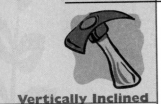

DAY 4

Fear of Heights ...
Avoiding High Places

Several years ago a friend confronted me about what she perceived to be pride in my life. At first I felt hurt. But I didn't want to dismiss her assessment if God was trying to correct me. I asked the Lord to teach me about pride and humility. I asked him to "poke me" with conviction whenever pride reared its ugly head in my spirit. I had a group of women specifically pray over me that I might be alert and on guard against pride.

I discovered I have a lot more pride in my heart than I thought. Pride is at the root of my impatience with slow traffic; my irritation with the incompetence of the teller at the store; my criticism of my relative's behavior; my sarcasm about people's lack of morality and intelligence; my fear of failure; my defensiveness when criticized; my desire for control; my unwillingness to take the first step toward reconciliation. Even when my actions and motives are honorable, they are not entirely free of pride. I can see a prideful thread—a "me-focus"—hidden in virtually everything I do and say.

Pride is a poison that affects all of our attitudes and actions. In fact, it could be argued that pride is the evil behind all other sins. This is illustrated in the life of Israel's first king, Saul. Saul had a volatile temper. He was suspicious of the motives of others and often jumped to conclusions. He was rash and impetuous in his decisions. He was competitive and jealous. He hated certain people. He didn't fully obey God. But though he had many faults, the prophet Samuel identified Saul's basic problem as arrogance (1 Sam. 15:23). All of Saul's sins were connected to the underlying evil of pride.

Read 1 Samuel 15:10-30. Explain why you think God likened Saul's attitude of arrogance to the evil of idolatry. (You may want to refer to day 1 of this week's lessons to help you answer this question.)

_____

_____

_____

Saul appeared very spiritual. But God saw Saul's heart. He saw that it was filled with pride. Saul was his own god—he idolized himself. That's why God rejected him as king that day in Gilgal. Find out more about Gilgal in today's High Point.

Honor and Dishonor: The Stones of Gilgal

Gilgal was the site of the Israelites' first encampment after crossing the Jordan into the promised land (Josh. 9:6). After arriving, the people renewed their covenant to God by circumcising all males born since leaving Egypt (Josh. 5:2). The place was named Gilgal (Heb., "rolling") for it was there God "rolled away the reproach of Egypt" (Josh. 5:9). Joshua instructed the Israelites to set up 12 memorial stones at Gilgal—one stone for each tribe—to remind them of the power of the Lord so they would always honor and obey Him (Josh. 4:24).

During the time of Judges, Gilgal was an important spiritual center. Samuel, the last judge of Israel, frequented the town on his yearly circuit, and offered priestly sacrifices there (1 Sam. 7:16; 10:8; 13:7-9). Gilgal was also important in the life of Israel's first king, Saul. After his initial military victory, the people of Israel gathered at Gilgal to affirm Saul's kingship (1 Sam. 11:14). Several years later, the kingship was taken from him for presumptuously performing a priestly ritual in Gilgal (1 Sam. 13:8-15). Ironically, Saul dishonored God in the very place the 12 memorial stones cast their shadows as reminders to honor Him.

Later in Israel's history, the people of Gilgal totally rejected God. They turned that holy place into a place dedicated to the worship of idols, prostitution, and adultery (Amos 4:4; 5:5; Hosea 4:15). The prophets condemned them for their arrogance and predicted their downfall (Hos. 5:5). The stones of Gilgal signify the principle that those who honor God are honored, and those who in pride dishonor Him, are dishonored. "A man's pride brings him low, but a man of lowly spirit gains honor" (Prov. 29:23).

"The true way to be humble is not to stoop until you are smaller than yourself, but to stand at your real height against some higher nature that will show you what the real smallness of your greatness is."
—Phillips Brooks[7]

A Tale of Two Kings

God determined to replace King Saul with a "man after his own heart" (1 Sam. 13:13-14). God's humility is most vividly seen in Jesus (Matt. 11:29).

When looking for "a man after his own heart" to be king, the Lord chose the shepherd boy, David. Saul's heart was proud. David's heart was humble. Their basic attitude affected their behavior and how they responded in various situations. The chart following compares the two.

Complete the chart on the following page by determining how you would most likely respond in each situation. Are you more like Saul or David? Check the box in the right-hand column to indicate your answer.

Situation	How did Saul respond?	How did David respond?	Who are you more like?
You've accomplished something great.	When Saul accomplished something great, his first response was to take credit. He wanted everybody to see how great he was (1 Sam. 15:12).	When David accomplished something great, his first response was to bow down and worship God. He wanted everyone to see how great God was (2 Sam. 22:47-49).	❑ Saul ❑ David
Your rival is praised and recognized and you are not.	Saul became angry and jealous when David received praise and recognition. He felt intimidated by David's accomplishments (1 Sam. 18:8,14).	David enjoyed seeing others promoted and recognized. He even praised and honored Saul when Saul treated him badly (2 Sam 1:23-24; 3:38).	❑ Saul ❑ David
Someone tells you that you are wrong.	When confronted, Saul became defensive, made excuses, and blamed others (1 Sam 15:15, 20,24).	When confronted, David listened, accepted personal responsibility, and humbly accepted correction (2 Sam. 12:13; 19:5-8; 24:10,17).	❑ Saul ❑ David
You've "blown it," and there's a chance that others will find out.	When his sin was discovered, Saul's primary concern was his reputation. He didn't want people to think badly of him. He tried to hide and gloss over his wrongdoing (1 Sam. 15:30).	When his sin was discovered, David's primary concern was making it right with God. He was more worried about what God thought than what people thought. He didn't try to hide his wrongdoing (2 Sam. 12; 24:17).	❑ Saul ❑ David
Someone close to you disappoints and/or betrays you.	Saul became angry and vindictive toward his son when Jonathan disappointed him. He held on to his grudge and didn't forgive (1 Sam. 20:30-33; 22:8).	David was eager to forgive and be reconciled when his son betrayed him. David took the first step toward restoring the relationship. He was grieved when Absalom was punished for his behavior (2 Sam. 13:37; 14:21; 18:33).	❑ Saul ❑ David
You are facing a crisis or difficult situation.	Saul impatiently took matters into his own hands—relying on his own wisdom and competence to solve the situation (1 Sam. 13:9-13; 22:17-19).	David strengthened himself in the Lord, inquired of the Lord, and patiently waited on the Lord to answer his prayers (1 Sam 30:6; Ps. 37:7).	❑ Saul ❑ David

Two Sides of Pride

Pride is subtle. It can disguise itself as a false form of humility. The apostle Paul argued that some people who appear very spiritual are, in fact, puffed up with pride. They delight in "false humility" (Col. 2:18).

When the prophet wanted to present King Saul to the people, Saul was nowhere to be found. He was hiding among the baggage, incapacitated by feelings of inadequacy (1 Sam. 9:21; 10:22). Initially, Saul's insecurities caused him to shy away from being king. Later those same insecurities caused him to promote himself, and to envy and pursue David, whom he perceived as a threat. Compare this to David, who humbly and willingly accepted God's calling on his life (1 Sam. 23:16-18). He never sought advancement, nor did he shy away from it when he perceived that God was advancing and honoring him (1 Sam. 18:23; 1 Chron 17:17-18).

Pride exists whenever I am focused on "me" instead of God. It can show up as self-exaltation or self-abasement, a false form of humility. Tomorrow we'll learn more about true humility. Finish today's lesson by putting on some Climbing Gear. Ask the Lord to teach you how to be humble like David.

"The meek man ... has accepted God's estimate of his own life. ... In himself, nothing; in God, everything. That is his motto."
—A. W. Tozer[8]

Sawdust and Planks

Prideful people focus on the "specks of sawdust" in other people's eyes and fail to see the "planks" in their own (Matt. 7:3). When you find yourself being critical, argumentative, or defensive, STOP. You're looking the wrong way. You need to move your eyes from looking down at others to looking up at God. Ask Him to help you identify the "plank" in your own eye. Resolve to deal with what He shows you before you criticize and correct the other person. If criticism is a big problem for you, you may want to put a piece of wood with Matthew 7:3 written on it in your purse or pocket every morning. You can't criticize until you've gotten rid of the "plank." You get rid of the plank through self-examination, prayer, and repentance. So when the urge to condemn comes, put off your criticism until you've dealt with your own "stuff." Do this consistently, and your habit of criticism will virtually disappear.

DAY 5

Before a Fall...
The Way Through High Places

"Young men, in the same way be submissive to those who are older. All of you, clothe yourselves with humility toward one another, because, 'God opposes the proud but gives grace to the humble' " (1 Pet. 5:5-6).

You might wonder if pursuing humility is not a contradiction in terms. Aren't those who think they are getting more humble actually getting more proud? What does the Bible say about growing in humility?

Read 1 Peter 5:5-6 in the margin. Circle the picture that best represents how we grow in humility.

Explain what you think is involved when you "clothe yourself with humility."

The habit of getting dressed begins in childhood and continues throughout our lives. Each morning, I take off my nightclothes and put on a fresh set of clothes. I'm sure you do the same thing.

The point of the verse is that humility doesn't just happen. It doesn't fall on us like rain on thirsty ground. Humility is something we actively and volitionally put on—like dressing ourselves in fresh clothes. Furthermore, it's important to realize it's not a one-time occurrence. We need to "put on" humility each day for the rest of our lives. It may be that we get better at it—and that it takes less effort—but the need to clothe ourselves in humility never ends. Thus, it's helpful to regard humility as an ongoing habit—a discipline—rather than a skill that is mastered.

"Should you ask me what is the first thing in religion, I should reply that the first, second, and third thing therein is humility."—Augustine[9]

To finish our study of the Mount of Appraisal, you're going to do a 20 question "Humility Check" to determine if there are areas in your life in which you need to clothe yourself with humility. Ask God to help you answer the questions honestly. If you're really brave, you may even ask your spouse or a friend to review them with you to give you additional feedback.

Humility Check

1. Do you boast about things you've done or possessions you've acquired? Are you concerned about making an impression? Do you feel envious when others have more than you? (Ps. 10:3, 27:2, 62:10).

❑ never   ❑ seldom   ❑ occasionally   ❑ often   ❑ habitually

2. Are you critical? Do you focus on the inadequacy and mistakes of others and mock or deride them for their shortcomings? Can you clearly see the log in other people's eyes? (Ps. 10:5-7; 73:6; Prov. 3:34, 21:24).

❑ never   ❑ seldom   ❑ occasionally   ❑ often   ❑ habitually

3. Are you self-abasing? Do you run yourself down and speak poorly of yourself? Do you want others to feel sorry for you and/or counter your negative self-talk with complements? (Prov. 25:27; Col. 2:18; James 1:9-10).

❑ never   ❑ seldom   ❑ occasionally   ❑ often   ❑ habitually

4. Do you like to "strut your feathers?" Do you want people to recognize that your abilities, knowledge, wit, and/or spirituality are superior? Do you feel pleased when you sense that you impress or intimidate them? (Ps. 10:7; Isa. 23:91; Jer. 49:16; 1 Cor. 4:6).

❑ never   ❑ seldom   ❑ occasionally   ❑ often   ❑ habitually

5. Are you quick to blame others? Do you become defensive when challenged or criticized? Are you slow to ask for forgiveness? Do you see the size of the other person's sin as bigger than your own and expect them to apologize first? (2 Kings 22:19; Prov. 6:2-3).

❑ never   ❑ seldom   ❑ occasionally   ❑ often   ❑ habitually

6. Do you gossip and slander? Do you secretly want other people's shortcomings to be exposed? Do you feel satisfied when others suffer the negative consequences of their behavior? Do you secretly want them to fail? Do you devise or participate in schemes to "catch" and trip them up? (Ps. 10:2; Prov. 8:13, 16:19).

❑ never   ❑ seldom   ❑ occasionally   ❑ often   ❑ habitually

7. Are you independent? Are you sassy, insolent, and/or disrespectful towards those who seek to give you input? Do you criticize leaders? (Prov. 13:1,13; 15:12; Isa. 16:6).

❑ never   ❑ seldom   ❑ occasionally   ❑ often   ❑ habitually

8. Are you insecure? Do you constantly wonder what others are thinking about you? Do you base your self-image on their opinion? Does fear of failure and/or fear of appearing foolish keep you from doing things? (Prov. 10:24; 15:33; 28:26; 29:25).

❑ never   ❑ seldom   ❑ occasionally   ❑ often   ❑ habitually

9. Are you easily provoked? When hurt, do you become infuriated, and attack and/or retaliate? Are you combative and argumentative? (Ps. 56:2; Prov. 9:7; 22:10; 29:22-23; Eccl. 7:9; Isa. 58:3-4).

❑ never   ❑ seldom   ❑ occasionally   ❑ often   ❑ habitually

10. Do you have a desire to be honored? Do you feel hurt or resentful when others are recognized or promoted and you are not? (Prov. 25:27; 27:2; Isa. 23:9; 26:5).

❑ never ❑ seldom ❑ occasionally ❑ often ❑ habitually

11. Do you cringe when you are recognized? Do you pull back and hide? Do you refuse to let others serve or help you? (Prov. 29:23,25; Matt. 23:12).

❑ never ❑ seldom ❑ occasionally ❑ often ❑ habitually

12. Do you deceive/mislead others about your abilities, accomplishments, and/or character? Do you present yourself as more spiritual than you are? Are you afraid to let others see the real you? Do you wear masks? (Prov. 11:1-2; 25:14).

❑ never ❑ seldom ❑ occasionally ❑ often ❑ habitually

13. Are you worried that your sins and failures will become known? Are you more concerned about damaging your reputation than about grieving God? Do you try to cover up and conceal your problems so others won't find out? (Prov. 9:8; 11:12; 15:12; 24:16).

❑ never ❑ seldom ❑ occasionally ❑ often ❑ habitually

14. Are you satisfied with your own spiritual condition? Do you have a hard time thinking of personal spiritual needs or sins to repent of? Are you convinced that it's not you, but everyone else, who needs spiritual renewal? (2 Chron. 7:14; Isa. 58:2-4; Dan. 5:20-21).

❑ never ❑ seldom ❑ occasionally ❑ often ❑ habitually

15. When spiritual matters are discussed, do you monopolize the conversation? Do you think your understanding about spiritual things is deeper than others? Do you feel the need to correct and challenge their understanding? (Prov. 26:12; Col. 2:18).

❑ never ❑ seldom ❑ occasionally ❑ often ❑ habitually

16. Are you resistant to change? Are you controlling? Do you use threats, half-truths, and/or manipulation to get your way? (Ps. 10:7; Prov. 8:13).

❑ never ❑ seldom ❑ occasionally ❑ often ❑ habitually

17. Do you fail to take time to think about or seek God? Are you unalarmed and unconcerned about your lack of spiritual passion? Do you feel complacent when it comes to obeying Scripture? (Ex. 10:3; Lev. 26:40-41; Deut 8:2; 2 Chron. 7:14; Ps. 10:4; Ps. 107:11).

❑ never ❑ seldom ❑ occasionally ❑ often ❑ habitually

18. Do you trust in your own competence and capabilities? Do you have a subconscious feeling that you have it "all together" and that groups and organizations are extremely lucky to have you participate and/or contribute? (Prov. 26:12; Isa. 9:9).

❑ never ❑ seldom ❑ occasionally ❑ often ❑ habitually

19. Do you shrink back from getting involved? Do you question that God could ever use you? Do you wallow in self-pity because He has given other people gifts and abilities you do not have? Are you incapacitated by feelings of inadequacy? (Rom.12:6-8; 1 Cor. 12:11; 1 Pet. 4:10).

❏ **never**   ❏ **seldom**   ❏ **occasionally**   ❏ **often**   ❏ **habitually**

20. Do you have a "why-don't-you-pull-up-your-socks" attitude towards those who have less skills and resources? Do you lack compassion? Is your heart callous? Are you unmoved by the plight of the disadvantaged, poor, and needy? (Ps. 73:6; Prov. 15:25; 29:7).

❏ **never**   ❏ **seldom**   ❏ **occasionally**   ❏ **often**   ❏ **habitually**

How did you do? It's not a test that many would pass with flying colors! But it does demonstrate that growing in humility is a lifetime project. God has a lot of work to do in each of us! The best way to make our way through High Places is to keep our eyes firmly fixed on Jesus, and to focus on His glory, beauty, and majesty.

Close this week's lessons by drawing lines to match the Scripture references to what they say about the greatness of God. When you're done, spend some time in prayer, worshiping Him.

"The tumult and the shouting dies, The captains and the kings depart; Still stands Thine ancient sacrifice, An humble and a contrite heart." —Rudyard Kipling[10]

Psalm 138:2
Psalm 97:9
Ephesians 1:21
Nehemiah 9:5
Psalm 108:5
Psalm 99:2

He's above all gods.
He's above all nations.
He's above the heavens.
He's above all things.
He's above all blessing and praise.
He's above all rule, authority, power, and dominion.

The Mount of Affliction
Godward Climbers Persevere Through Difficulty

af•flic•tion—a state of acute pain or distress of body or mind; to trouble, to grieve; to harass; to torment; to distress. Have you ever faced difficulty? Every road has its ups and downs. The goal of this week's study is to challenge you to keep going when the going gets tough.

Base Camp
OK, so it's not the Tour de France, but it is a tough ride! In this week's Base Camp we'll be cycling through the mountains to learn more about how to keep going when we face big hills in life. The writer of Hebrews gave the believers in Italy some great advice on how to persevere through difficulty and make it to the top.

Daily Lessons
Day 1: Uphill Battle
… Expecting Ups and Downs
Day 2: Champion of the Hill
… Following the King of the Mountain
Day 3: Burning Uphill
… Transforming Pain to Gain
Day 4: Cleft of the Hill
… Running for Cover
Day 5: Over the Hill
… Persevering to the End

High Points
- Valley of Rephaim
- The Kidron Valley
- Valley of Achor
- Cave of Adullam
- Valley of Baca

Climbing Gear
- Going for Gold
- Blind Trust

Memory Pack
"Shout for joy, O heavens; rejoice, O earth; burst into song, O mountains! For the LORD comforts his people and will have compassion on his afflicted ones" (Isa. 49:13).

The Mount of Affliction: Straining Uphill
Hebrews 12:1-13

Summit 4—

The Mount of Affliction

This Base Camp Guide will help you follow the video session for Summit 4.

1. Precarious Perspective

a. *Life should be easy.* (v. 1)
Hardships are a part of every _____.

b. *God doesn't care.* (v. 6)
Hardships are an _____ of His love.

c. *I'm being punished.* (v. 5-11)
Hardships are God's _____ _____.

d. *I don't deserve this.* (v. 2,5)
Through hardships we _____ in the life of Christ.

2. Precarious Preoccupation

a. *It's too big.* (v. 4—magnitude)
Hardships are _____ in light of the _____ of God.

b. *It's too painful!* (v. 11—intensity)
Hardships are _____ in light of their _____ _____.

c. *It's lasting too long!* (v. 10—duration)
Hardships are _____ in light of God's _____ purpose.

3. Precarious Position

a. _____ up (v. 3,5—don't become weary and lose heart, discouraged).

b. _____ up (v. 1—hindrances and sin entanglements).

c. _____ up (v. 12-13—choosing disability).

When hardships come, keep pushing upward. Fix your eyes on Jesus and run with perseverance. That's the way to conquer the Mount of Affliction.

75

Vertically Inclined

DAY 1

Uphill Battle ...
Expecting Ups and Downs

It took a few moments before I noticed the lights and siren of the police cruiser. My eyes were blurred with tears and my mind was definitely not on driving. I pulled over as soon as I got across the Low Level Bridge. "Low Level"—an apt description for that period of my life. Earlier that morning, at the children's hospital, life had dealt me another bitter blow. The speeding violation merely added insult to injury.

License. Registration. I retrieved the necessary documents in a detached fog. I could feel the painful knot twisting from my sternum to the back of my throat. It felt as though my innards had been wrung like a dishrag and crammed in a tight wad behind my ribs. Breathe. Breathe. Don't fall apart now. I put my hand under my nose to stave off the flood.

"Are you all right?" The irony of the question almost amused me. All right? A business crisis, lawsuit, miscarriage of twins, health issues, church conflict, family stress, husband with ruptured appendix, broken bones, a critically ill child, and now another child diagnosed with facing a lifetime of being deaf. I can't plug all the holes in the dike! The wall is crumbling ... waves and breakers are crashing over me ... I'm thrashing about but can't keep my head above water! Am I all right???!!! What kind of a stupid question is that? I nod feebly and mumble something as the officer hands me the ticket.

"The real problem is not why some pious, humble, believing people suffer, but why some do not."
—C.S. Lewis[1]

"Have a good day, now!"—a kind refrain, but it felt more like a parting shot. The cruiser pulled away. Day? Is it really day? It seems like night. Every day lately seems like night. What day is it, anyhow? I look down at the pink slip of paper in my hand: April 1, 1992 ... April Fools'. I can no longer hold back. The screams and tears erupt in a torrent as I pound the wheel with both fists. It's just not fair! I'm the fool on the receiving end of an incredibly cruel cosmic joke. "Why—oh, God—WHY?"

The "Why" Question

When we face disappointments, hardships, and tragedies, we want to know why we are facing them, and why—if He indeed loves us—God doesn't intervene to resolve them in the way we would like. The "why" question is probably the most frequently asked question in the history of mankind.

In the following list, read the questions that some prominent biblical figures asked of God. In each question, circle the word *why*.

People of Israel:	Why is my way hidden from the LORD? Why does He disregard my cause? (Isa. 40:27). "Why has this happened to me?" (Jer. 13:22).
David:	"Why have you rejected me? Why must I go about mourning, oppressed by the enemy?" (Ps. 43:2). "Why … [do you] hide your face from me?" (Ps. 88:14).
Isaiah:	"Why, O LORD, do you make us wander from your ways and harden our hearts so we do not revere you?" (Isa. 63:17).
Jeremiah:	"Why did I ever come out of the womb to see trouble and sorrow and to end my days in shame?" (Jer. 20:18).
Habakkuk:	"Why then do you tolerate the treacherous? Why are you silent while the wicked swallow up those more righteous than themselves?" (Hab. 1:13).
Jesus:	"My God, my God, why have you forsaken me?" (Mark 15:34).

Do any of these questions surprise you? ❑ yes ❑ no **Explain your answer in the margin.**

It surprises me that Jesus would ask, "Why?" He, more than anyone, was acquainted with the Father's plan. Yet in His suffering and death, Jesus experienced acute physical and mental pain and the unspeakable horror of separation from God, and he, too, cried out, "Why?"

My friend, Rusty, suffered through cancer. He maintains that the "why" question is not a question that expects an answer. It's more of a rhetorical cry lamenting the fractured, broken state of a world crippled by evil. As the song writer, Bruce Cockburn, says, we live in "a world that never was"—a place "where the questions are all 'why' and the answers are all 'because.' "[2] There's a certain enigma to the human condition and the fact of human suffering.

Why do good and evil exist? Why do we reject God? Why do we choose evil? Why, without God's help, are we powerless to do what is right? Why do we face sickness and death? Why do bad things happen to good people? When it comes down to it, there's no easy answer for the question, "Why?"

Suffering is a fact of life—particularly for followers of Christ. Peter advised the believers scattered across the region, "Do not be surprised at the painful trial you are suffering, as though something strange were happening to you" (1 Pet. 4:12). The recipients of his letter were perplexed about the difficulties they were facing. They thought a relationship with Jesus meant immunity from suffering. But the Bible teaches that's just not the case.

Read these verses and match each reference to the thought it presents.

Job 5:7   **Don't be unsettled by trials— you are destined for them.**

2 Timothy 3:12   **In this world you will have trouble.**

1 Thessalonians 3:3   **You must go through many hardships to enter the kingdom of God.**

John 16:33   **Everyone who wants to live a godly life will be persecuted.**

Acts 14:22   **You will experience trouble as surely as sparks fly upwards.**

Psalm 34:19   **You may experience many troubles.**

David said, "A righteous man may have many troubles, but the LORD delivers him from them all" (Ps. 34:19). David ought to have known. During the course of his lifetime, he faced one giant-sized problem after another. Read more about his troubles in today's High Point on page 79.

Have you faced "giant hills" in your life? On the picture of the mountain, list some difficult situations you have faced or are now facing.

With regards to these difficult situations, have you ever asked "why"? ❑ yes ❑ no ❑ I'm not sure.

Changing the Question

There's nothing wrong with asking "Why?" Some of the godliest people in the Bible did. But as my friend Rusty said, it's not a question that expects an answer. He proposes that instead of asking "Why me?" sufferers ask, "What now?" "Why me?" is a question borne of frustration; "What now?" is a

One Giant Problem After Another: Valley of Rephaim

David was just a boy when he killed Goliath with a stone from a sling (1 Sam. 17). Goliath was a descendent of the Rephaim, a fierce race of giants who were the original inhabitants of the land of Canaan. During the time of Abraham, the Rephaim were defeated and dispersed by an alliance of armies (Gen. 14:5). Some time later, the Philistines —a group of sea people from the Greek island of Crete—invaded the land. The surviving Rephaim settled among the Philistines and often fought as Philistine champions.

The Rephaim were a formidable people. The Israelites were intimidated by their sheer size and strength—describing themselves as "grasshoppers" in comparison (Num. 13:32-33). Goliath was over 9 feet tall. Og, King of Bashan, was so tall that he slept in an iron bed 13 feet long and 6 feet wide (Deut. 3:11). Another massive Rephaim had 6 fingers on each hand and 6 toes on each foot (1 Chron. 20:6). The Rephaim's weapons were also intimidating. Goliath's armor, made of polished plates of bronze, weighed 125 pounds. He sported a spear as thick as a man's thigh (1 Sam. 17:5-7).

After defeating Goliath, David faced one giant after another (1 Chron. 20:4-6; 2 Sam. 21:15-22). Many of these battles were fought in the Valley of Rephaim (the valley of the giants), a broad, fertile plain 3 or 4 miles southwest of Jerusalem (2 Sam. 5:18,22). Near the end of his life, exhausted from fighting, David was almost killed by the giant, Ishbi-Benob (2 Sam. 21:15-22). But with God's help, he and his men rallied to defeat the last of the Rephaim.

David faced more than 50 years of "giant-sized" problems. His conclusion? "A righteous man may have many troubles, but the LORD delivers him from them all" (Ps. 34:19).

"But under them all there runs a loud perpetual wail, as of souls in pain." —Henry Wadsworth Longfellow[3]

question filled with expectation. "Why me?" anguishes over why a situation happened; "What now?" anticipates what God will do next.

David often asked, "What now?" When he faced giant problems, he looked for what God was doing. ("Would you let my father and mother come and stay with you until I learn what God will do for me?" [1 Sam. 22:3].) Focusing on the *what* instead of the *why* filled him with hope.

This week we're going to focus on *what?* rather than *why?* I think you'll discover the answers are much more satisfying. And I think you'll come to understand why Peter said, "In this you greatly rejoice, though now for a little while you may have had to suffer grief in all kinds of trials" (1 Pet. 1:6).

Vertically Inclined

DAY 2

Champion of the Hill ...

Following the King of the Mountain

On July 27, 2003, Lance Armstrong cycled the last leg over the cobble-stoned Les Champs Elysees to claim the title in the century-old Tour de France—cycling's most brutal and prestigious race. The win—his fifth consecutive—tied a Tour de France record and established him as one of the greatest cyclists of all time. Armstrong overcame illness, crashes, inclement weather, and an array of determined opponents to secure the victory.

Armstrong possesses extraordinary athletic talent and strength, but Sally Jenkins, coauthor of his autobiographies, says that it's his ability to suffer that truly sets him apart.[4] This trait was learned during his fight with cancer. In 1996, doctors discovered a testicular cancer so advanced it had spread to his lungs and brain. Though the prognosis was not good, Armstrong determinedly fought through surgery and aggressive chemotherapy to return to the sport he loved. Armstrong maintains that the cancer was an unexpected gift— "the best thing that ever happened to me."[5] It taught him how to suffer, and brought maturity and focus to his life. Now, suffering is as important to him as happiness. "It's not a good day if I haven't suffered a little," he says.[6]

It's Armstrong's willingness to suffer that makes him one of the best hill-climbing cyclists in the world. During a climb, his eyes go completely bloodshot. The effort he exerts is severe enough to burst all the capillaries. "I have the will to suffer," Armstrong admits, "I do have that."[7] And that's the quality that makes him a winner. It's not that he enjoys suffering for pain's sake. It's just that he sees it as an integral part of reaching a greater goal. In the final analysis, it's the magnetism of the finish line that motivates him. The awaiting prize is what gives him the will to suffer.[8]

The Magnetism of the Finish Line

My husband, Brent, was a national track and field gold medalist. I remember being amazed at his will to push beyond the limits of physical comfort. In training, he would run so hard that he'd be sick and vomit into a bucket he had positioned beside the track for that very purpose. He knew ahead of time how awful the workout would feel, and he hated the thought of it, but he did it anyway. Like every other elite athlete, Brent was motivated by "the magnetism of the finish line."

Jesus was "a man of sorrows, and familiar with suffering" (Isa. 53:3). He had a greater "will to suffer" than any elite athlete ever did. Why? What motivated the Son of God to willingly "empty himself," be born as a human, suffer, and die a brutal death?

80

Read Hebrews 12:2-3 in the margin. Explain why you think Jesus had the will to suffer.

"Let us fix our eyes on Jesus, the author and perfecter of our faith, who for the joy set before him endured the cross, scorning its shame, and sat down at the right hand of the throne of God. Consider him who endured such opposition from sinful men, so that you will not grow weary and lose heart" (Heb. 12:2-3).

Many martyrs have died gruesome deaths. But their suffering doesn't even begin to compare to the sufferings of Christ. The indignity of the disdain, rejection, torture, and violence Jesus suffered was exponentially magnified by the fact that He, the Creator, was being abused by the very ones He created. It's rather like the unfathomable situation of a father being taunted, tortured, and murdered by his toddler. When you take a moment to think about it, it's beyond belief! What makes Christ's sufferings particularly remarkable is that at any moment He could have stopped them. " 'Do you think I cannot call on my Father, and he will at once put at my disposal more than twelve legions of angels? But how then would the Scriptures be fulfilled?' " (Matt. 26:53-54).

Not only did Jesus need to bear up under the scorn and pain that came His way, He also needed to resist the temptation to use His power to stop it. In the Garden of Gethsemane His anguish over this decision was so great that His sweat was like drops of blood falling to the ground. The prospect of the cross was deeply distressing, but in the end, the magnetism of the finish line gave Him the will to suffer. He endured the pain of that daunting hill "for the joy set before him" (Heb. 12:2).

The path to Gethsemane and the cross was not a garden path. Read more about it in today's High Point.

Not a Garden Path: The Kidron Valley

Gethsemane was an olive garden on the western slopes of the Mount of Olives. It was a favorite retreat frequented by Christ and His disciples. It was also the place where Jesus prayed in lonely anguish just before His betrayal, arrest, and subsequent crucifixion. To get to Gethsemane from Jerusalem, it was necessary to cross the Kidron Valley, which lies between the Temple Mount and the Mount of Olives.

The Kidron Valley is a torrent-bed with precipitous, rocky banks. During the rainy season, water flows in a stream through the bottom of the valley. But for most of the year, it's dry and sun baked—attested to by its modern name: _"Wadi en-Nar,"_ ravine of fire. Its Hebrew name, _Cedron_, means "turbid" or "troubled."

This valley of fire was the scene of much trouble. King David crossed the Kidron barefooted and weeping after being betrayed by his son, Absalom

81

(2 Sam. 15:23,30). It was here where the reforming kings, such as Asa, Hezekiah, and Josiah destroyed the pagan idols with which the people had prostituted themselves (1 Kings 15:13; 2 Kings 23:6; 2 Chron. 29:16; 30:14). By the time of King Josiah, the banks of the valley were used as a burial site for commoners (2 Kings 23:6). And by Christ's time, memorial tombs such as the Pillar of Absalom, the Cave of Jehoshaphat, the Tomb of Bene Hezier, and the Tomb of Zachariah had been built there. The Kidron Valley was prophetically referred to as "the valley of decision" (Joel 3:14). It's the place where God will judge the multitudes for the decisions they have made.

Perhaps all these thoughts passed through Christ's mind as He made His way to Gethsemane that night. What would He do? What decision would He make? Was He willing to be obedient to His Father even if it meant excruciating pain? Was He willing to walk through this dark valley and up the steep hill? Did He have the will to suffer? It was the ultimate test. He could have chosen the garden path. But for the joy set before Him, Jesus chose the path of the cross. He pushed hard through the pain, crossed the finish line in victory, and become the champion of salvation.

"You must submit to supreme suffering in order to discover the completion of joy."—John Calvin[9]

Jesus was well aware of what it would take to become the champion of salvation. Scripture foretold His sufferings. Look up the verses. Describe the afflictions they prophesied Christ would suffer.

Psalm 22:6-8;13-18 _____

_____

Psalm 69:7-9;19-21 _____

_____

Isaiah 53:2-5;7-10 _____

_____

Read the following passage that describes what Jesus did and didn't do when facing the pain of unjust suffering:

"It is commendable if a man bears up under the pain of unjust suffering because he is conscious of God ...To this you were called, because Christ suffered for you, leaving you an example, that you should follow in his steps. 'He committed no sin, and no deceit was found in his mouth.' When they hurled their insults at him, he did not retaliate; when he suffered, he made no threats. Instead, he entrusted himself to him who judges justly. He himself bore our sins in his body on the tree, so that we might die to sins and live for righteousness; by his wounds you have been healed" (1 Pet. 2:19,21-24).

In the passage above, circle five phrases that describe how Christ responded to suffering. Now underline the sentence, "Christ suffered for you, leaving you an example, that you should follow in his steps."

How do you react when you suffer unjustly? Check all that apply.

❑ Look for a way to end the pain and make the suffering stop.
❑ "Bite the bullet" to prove how tough I am.
❑ Retaliate and make threats against my opponents.
❑ Hurl insults and slander those who have hurt me.
❑ Lick my wounds and become incapacitated with self-pity.
❑ Put up emotional walls and hide behind masks.
❑ Get angry and question why God would allow the situation to continue.
❑ Follow the example of Jesus.

What do you think it means to "entrust yourself" to God when suffering? Write your thoughts in the margin.

"He who fears to suffer cannot be His who suffered."—Tertullian[10]

Champion of Suffering
This side of heaven we may never fully understand why we suffer. But Scripture certainly gives us crystal clear direction on how to act in the face of suffering. Jesus, our champion, left us an example. Are you facing a steep hill of affliction? You can be assured that His treads have already marked the route. He's been there. He's conquered that hill. And with His help, you too can make it to the top. Close today's lesson by asking the champion of suffering to give you the will to follow His example and persevere though difficulty.

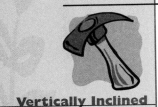

DAY 3

Burning Uphill ...
Transforming Pain to Gain

On one of the last few days of filming the *Vertically Inclined* video, the air was so hazy that we could hardly see the mountains in the background. Smoke from forest fires had blown into the area and substantially reduced visibility. In the weeks following the film shoot, lightening strikes ignited hundreds of new fires, and the situation worsened. The provincial government declared a state of emergency. The fires in the mountains were out of control. Homes burned to the ground. Multitudes were evacuated from towns and cities. Highways were closed—vacations cancelled. Droves of military personnel and volunteers were recruited to join the thousands of weary firefighters who battled the blazes. Several firefighters lost their lives. The fires were the worst on record. They destroyed more than two hundred thousand acres of forest in and around the Canadian Rockies.

The concern with the fires in the mountains is ultimately not the damage to the forests, but the damage to man-made structures, tourism, and the local economy. From a long-term perspective, fires are actually good for the lodgepole pine forests. The cones of these pines have a waxy resin coating. They lie sealed-up and dormant until the coating is "melted" by intense heat. Fire causes the cones to pop open and release their seeds onto soil that has been richly fertilized by nutrients in the fire's ash. The flames also clear away all the fallen and dying trees and rotting debris accumulated on the forest floor, leaving large patches of cleared ground open to the sun. This allows fresh young lodgepole seedlings and other plants to take root and flourish. Thus, the forest is rejuvenated and sustained. Without fire, lodgepole pine forests would stagnate and die out. Fires are a necessary part of their cycle of life.

Refiner's Fire
Peter likened trials to fire. "Do not be surprised at the fiery trial when it comes upon you to test you, as though something strange were happening to you" (1 Pet. 4:12, ESV). The Greek word translated, "fiery," is *purosis*.

You're going to play Scrabble™ to learn more about what *fiery* means. Use all the letters on the rack to add a word to the board. Hint: The word starts with a *P* and is related to the Greek word used in 1 Peter 4:12.

Your total points should be 60 (plus 50 more for using all your letters).

Gold is

_____

by fire.

Faith is proved

_____

by fire.

Refer to 1 Peter 1:6-7 to fill in the blanks in the margin.

In its natural state, gold is contaminated with the oxides of other metals. The impurities are removed by heating the gold in a crucible in a fiery furnace to temperatures greater than 1000 degrees Celsius. The molten gold collects in the bottom of the crucible while the waste product, called slag, accumulates on the surface. When the mass is cooled, the brittle slag can be broken off, leaving a cake of refined gold behind.

Peter claims that like gold, our faith is refined by fire. Fire purifies. (Did you add the word *purifies* to the scrabble board? *Purosis* refers to a fire that purifies.) The fires of trials refine and purify me, and prove that my faith is genuine. The trials themselves are only temporary, whereas my faith is eternal. That's why God regards the valley of trouble as a door of hope. Read more about the door of hope in today's High Point.

Door of Hope: Valley of Achor

Things were going well for the nation Israel. God had given them a spectacular victory at Jericho. In confidence, they turned their sight on their next goal: the city of Ai. Much to their surprise and dismay, Israel was humiliated in battle. The warriors of Ai struck down dozens of Israelites on the slopes as the Israelites fled in terror. The cause of their defeat soon became apparent. There was sin in the camp. Someone had taken forbidden booty (gold, silver, and a costly Babylonian garment) from Jericho. As a result of one person's sin, the whole nation suffered (Josh. 7).

The transgression came to light in the Valley of Achor (Heb., trouble, disturbance), a grassy bowl between Jericho and the north end of the Dead Sea. Joshua gathered the people there to deal with the problem. Lot by lot the crime was exposed. Under Joshua's direction, the wrongdoer, his family, his possessions, and the booty were all burned, and a large heap of rocks piled up as a reminder. The expression "Valley of Achor" subsequently became proverbial for trouble and calamity. Someone facing difficulty could say, "I'm walking through the Valley of Achor."

The prophet Hosea taught that for those who follow God's lead, the Valley of Achor is "a door of hope" (Hos. 2:15). Isaiah agreed. He maintained that God transforms calamity into a source of blessing. The Valley of Achor will be "a resting place for herds, for my people who seek me" (Isa. 65:10). With God, we are never trapped in a hopeless situation. He always opens a door.

"No pain, no palm; no thorns, no throne; no gall, no glory; no cross, no crown."—William Penn[11]

Trouble may come upon us because of our own sin, because of someone else's sin, or just because. In the end, it really doesn't matter why, for our response is basically the same. In the crucible of suffering, we must hold on to God, follow Him, and deal with any "slag" we see rising to the surface of our hearts. If we do this, our valley of trouble will become a door of hope. God will lead us through the dark valley and up to the top of the mountain.

Trouble brings out the best and the worst in people. I've faced many and varied trials in life. And I've noticed that whenever I'm in the crucible of suffering, all kinds of "slag"—impatience, bitterness, anger, pride, self-sufficiency, hypocrisy, despair, and doubt—rise up in my spirit. Impurities of my heart that remain hidden when life is easy become glaringly evident when life is hard. I've seen the ugliness of sin rear its head in times of trouble, but I've also seen God begin to remove those impurities and refine my faith.

In day 1 I referred to the day my youngest son, Jonathan, was diagnosed as severely hearing impaired. There was a great deal of difficulty and turmoil during that period in my life. The only thing I could do was throw myself into the arms of God. I fasted and prayed—not just for a few days, but week after week, month after month, and year after year. Suffering taught me the discipline of prayer and fasting. It taught me how to live in a constant state of spiritual dependency. It deepened my faith and my confidence in the goodness of God. It deepened my perseverance and my joy. I learned how to rest in God. I learned to love and forgive. I learned self-control. Here's my conclusion about that difficult time: in the end, the "gold" left in the bottom of the crucible is of far greater value than the pain I suffered in the fire.

Peter acknowledges that suffering is indeed painful. But he argues that the fiery pain is only temporary—the gold, on the other hand, is forever. And in this we can rejoice. God transforms our pain to gain.

Think about trials you have experienced or are currently experiencing. On the chart following, try to identify the gold and the slag of that particular crucible of suffering (if you need some ideas, look back through the past few paragraphs to see the gold and slag I identified from my time of trial).

Gold	Slag (Impurities)

We hurt when we go through suffering's crucible. For some, the pain is so excruciating it defies description. But those who are able to shift their attention from *why* to *what* are much more likely to get some satisfactory answers. We may not understand why God is allowing us to suffer, but if we look carefully, we may see what He is accomplishing in us through the process.

Most people go through difficulty, but only some are refined by it. When you face difficulty, do you slough off the slag and go for the gold? Read more about going for the gold in today's Climbing Gear.

"God says to man: 'With thy very wounds I will heal thee.' "
—*The Talmud*[12]

Going for Gold

In yesterday's lesson we talked about how cyclist Lance Armstrong's will to suffer makes him one of the best hill climbing cyclists in the world. It's the magnetism of the finish line that motivates him to endure the pain. Do you resent suffering? Or do you push through pain to go for the gold?

When you feel the heat, look for both the gold and the slag in your heart. Nurture the former and slough off the latter. It may be helpful to draw two columns on a piece of paper with the headings "gold" and "slag" to evaluate your situation. Ask the Holy Spirit to help you discern what He's doing in your life. Cooperate with Him. Allow the fire to refine and change you.

God guarantees those who suffer well will cross the finish line in glory. Ultimately, our suffering will "result in praise, glory and honor when Jesus Christ is revealed" (1 Peter 1:7). Victory is assured for those who go for the gold.

Meditate on Paul's words of encouragement in 2 Corinthians 4:16-18. If the Holy Spirit brings any thoughts to mind, write them in the margin.

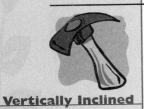

Vertically Inclined

Cleft of the Hill ...
Running for Cover

Without warning, the Gestapo stormed the Ten Boom Horologerie, the quaint clock shop situated on the ground floor of a home in the sleepy Dutch town of Haarlem. The guests upstairs knew the drill. They quickly snatched their plates and disappeared without a trace into the "hiding place"—an area behind a false wall in the bedroom. An intensive search of the house yielded some underground information and extra food ration cards, but not what the Gestapo sought most. The Nazis hauled the Ten Boom family off to jail, but two Jewish men, two Jewish women, and two members of the Dutch underground remained safely hidden in the walls of the house.

Corrie Ten Boom and her sister, Betsie, soon found themselves in Ravensbruck, the infamous concentration camp located near Berlin, Germany. The conditions were deplorable, the suffering immense. Their barrack stood in the shadow of the gas chambers and crematorium. The smokestacks regularly belched out the remains of those who had succumbed to the camp's horrors as well as those who were merely deemed unfit to live. It was here, surrounded by suffering and death, that Corrie and Betsie learned to run to another hiding place. They hid themselves in the arms of Jesus, and found comfort there. "There is no pit so deep," Corrie later explained, "that God's love is not deeper still."[13]

"Rock of Ages, cleft for me, let me hide myself in Thee."
—Augustus M. Toplady[14]

A Place of Refuge

When I was a little girl and faced the prospect of the pain of discipline, I used to run and hide in the closet. When danger looms, our first instinct is to run and hide. The guests in the Ten Boom house ran and took refuge in a hiding place behind the wall. In that place, they were safe from their enemies. But what do we do when there's nothing to shelter or protect us from difficulty? Where do we turn when there's no hiding place in sight?

David has a word of advice for those who are troubled and distressed. Write Psalm 9:9 in the margin. In the verse you just wrote, circle the words *refuge* and/or *stronghold*.

Did you circle two words? The noun translated *refuge* and/or *stronghold* (Heb., *Misgab*) is used twice in this verse. It's derived from a root that means, "to be high." It suggests security and protection in a high, safe place of retreat. The allusion is to the high, fortified towers, forts, or outposts that were common to the ancient world. According to Scripture, God is our stronghold. In times of trouble, we should run to Him.

The Bible uses other metaphors for this place of refuge. Under each reference, draw a picture of what God's place of refuge is like.

• Psalm 36:7 •

• Psalm 3:3 •

• Isaiah 51:16 •

• Psalm 94:22 •

God promises that in times of trouble He will shelter us under His wings, surround us with His shield, cover us with the shadow of His hand, and be our strong fortress—the rock in whom we can take refuge. Read more about the Rock of Refuge in today's High Point.

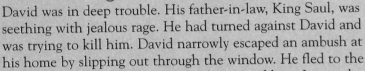

Rock of Refuge: Cave of Adullam

David was in deep trouble. His father-in-law, King Saul, was seething with jealous rage. He had turned against David and was trying to kill him. David narrowly escaped an ambush at his home by slipping out through the window. He fled to the prophet Samuel's town, but Saul and his men hotly pursued him. It was clear to David that he would not be safe in the urban centers of Israel. There was only one thing to do—head for the hills!

David headed toward the Judea mountains near the Philistine border. The region, situated about six miles southwest of Bethlehem, was well suited for his purpose. The limestone rock was honeycombed with numerous caverns. It was an ideal place to hide. Here, he took refuge in the cave of Adullam. After setting up camp, David was joined by his brothers, and hundreds of other men who were distressed, discontented, or in debt—men who were also seeking a place of rest (see 1 Sam. 22:1-2).

The word *Adullam* means, "refuge," "resting place," or "retreat." The stronghold of Addulam provided David a measure of safety and rest, but even more secure was the other refuge David hid himself in: the stronghold of God. While in the cave he prayed, "I cry to you, O Lord; I say 'You are my refuge' " (Ps. 142:5).

David's psalms are filled with references of God as a stronghold, a rock, a fortress, and a refuge. Many of them were written when David was on the run and forced to take refuge in caves, fortresses, and other strongholds. Yet even after he was king, and safe within the walls of the palace, David continued to make a habit of taking refuge in God. He hid himself in God whenever he faced difficulty. He said, "The Lord is a refuge for the oppressed, a stronghold in times of trouble. Those who know your name will trust in you, for you, Lord, have never forsaken those who seek you" (Ps. 9:9-10).

"It is such a comfort to drop the tangles of life into God's hands and leave them there."—C.E. Cowman[15]

When you face difficulties, do you take refuge in God? Do you rest in His hiding place? Or do you worry and fret about your situation? Mark an "x" on the scale below to indicate how you normally respond to trials.

| 0 | 1 | 2 | 3 | 4 | 5 | 6 | 7 | 8 | 9 | 10 |

I worry and fret.   I rest in the stronghold of God.

Whenever David was troubled or in anguish, he cried out to God. Read what he said in Psalm 118:5-9,13-14 in the margin.

Why was David unafraid when he faced difficulty?

_____

_____

_____

"In my anguish I cried to the LORD, and he answered by setting me free. The LORD is with me; I will not be afraid. What can man do to me? The LORD is with me; he is my helper. I will look in triumph on my enemies. It is better to take refuge in the LORD than to trust in man. It is better to take refuge in the LORD than to trust in princes ... I was pushed back and about to fall, but the LORD helped me. The LORD is my strength and my song; he has become my salvation" (Ps. 118:5-9,13-14).

According to the verses you just read, how did God answer David's cry for help? Check all that apply:

❑ He took David out of the difficult situation.
❑ He destroyed all of David's enemies.
❑ He made the enemies apologize and become friends.
❑ He helped David view the situation from a different perspective.
❑ He increased David's trust and faith.
❑ He helped David and gave him the strength to face the difficulty.
❑ He set David free from the bondage of stress and fear.
❑ He gave David joy and hope.

In the Psalm passage, circle the phrase: "He answered by setting me free."

God didn't take David out of the difficult situation, destroy his enemies, or make the enemies apologize and become friends. But he did deliver David from the oppressiveness of the situation by setting him "free." Did you check all but the first three boxes?

Hiding Place

One might explain to a child all the medical reasons why he must have a shot in the arm, but when he feels the sting of the needle, he simply looks for refuge in his mother's embrace. Comfort doesn't always come in knowing the reason why, or in knowing the outcome of the situation. It comes in running and taking refuge in the arms of the comforter.

Are you facing a difficult or stressful situation? There is a hiding place where you can be free from worry, stress, doubt, and fear. There is a Comforter in whose arms you can find rest. Close today's lesson by surrendering your worries and fears to Jesus, and praying this prayer of David: "You are my hiding place; you will protect me from trouble and surround me with songs of deliverance" (Ps. 32:7).

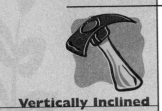

DAY 5

Over the Hill ...
Persevering to the End

Vertically Inclined

Friends of mine organize an annual cycling trip through the Canadian Rockies. The journey begins in Jasper and ends, five days later, in Banff. Each rider has a schedule that outlines the route, the distance between landmarks, and the next designated meeting point. Each day there are two destinations of prime importance: the lunch site, and the supper site (also where the group camps for the night). Volunteers in supply vehicles drive ahead and prepare the sites for our arrival. Cyclists know that refreshments will be waiting.

I've ridden the route several times, and sometimes the only thing that keeps me cycling is the knowledge that lunch is waiting for me just a few miles down the road. My ultimate goal is making it all the way to Banff. But my immediate goal is just surviving until I reach the site of our next meal.

Going from Strength to Strength

Read Psalm 84:5-7. These people were also on a journey. Match each question with the correct answer.

Where is their final destination?	springs and pools
What do they have to pass through to get there?	Mount Zion
Where can they stop for rest and refreshment?	pilgrimage
What one word describes the journey they are on?	meet God
What is the purpose of this journey?	God's strength
What is needed for this journey?	Valley of Baca

The travelers on this journey were on a pilgrimage. A pilgrimage is a journey made to a sacred place as an act of devotion. Historically, Jews traveled to Jerusalem three times a year to celebrate the traditional feasts: the Feast of Unleavened Bread (Passover), the Feast of Weeks (Pentecost), and the Feast of Booths (Deut. 16:16; Ex. 23:13-17; 34:18-23).

These verses depict the pilgrims passing through the Valley of Baca, also known as the Valley of Weeping. Journeys to feasts in Jerusalem were occasions of great joy, not weeping. Pilgrims reveled and sang Songs of Ascent as they approached (Isa. 30:29; Ps. 24,118,120–134). But the image here is one of difficulty, not revelry. These travelers needed the strength of God to make it. They only persevered by going from pool to pool—from strength to strength. Read more about the Valley of Baca in today's High Point.

Valley of Baca

To get to Mount Zion, pilgrims needed to pass through the Valley of Baca (Ps. 84:6). The word *Baca* is derived from the verb "to drip." It's the name of a balsam (mulberry) shrub, which grows in arid conditions and drips sap profusely when it's cut. Because of this imagery, the ancients traditionally referred to the Valley of Baca as the "Valley of Weeping" or the "Valley of the Weeper." It may have also been so called because it was lined with tombs.

The valley was apparently a very dry, waterless place. Only occasionally did small pools form and provide the parched ground reprieve.

A pilgrimage to the place where God dwells is a difficult journey. But God will provide abundant "pools" of blessing along the way. In Him, pilgrims will find the power to go from pool to pool—"from strength to strength"—until the day they reach their ultimate destination.

> "God washes the eyes by tears until they can behold the invisible land where tears shall come no more."
> —Henry Ward Beecher[16]

Figuratively, the New Testament portrays the entire Christian life as a pilgrimage toward Zion, where we will dwell with God for eternity (Heb. 11:13-16; 1 Pet. 1:17; 2:11). We will walk through the Valley of Weeping on the way, but even so, we can rejoice because we're headed for the place where Jesus will wipe every tear from our eyes. There will be no more death, mourning, crying, or pain (Rev. 21:4). It's the hope of glory that gladdens our hearts as we walk through difficult valleys.

The Hope of Glory

Suffering is like the first tile in a chain of dominos—it leads to several other things. Use the verses in the margin to fill in the blanks beside the dominos, indicating the sequence suffering triggers.

It seems ironic that suffering ultimately leads to hope. But the Bible teaches that this is the case. Hope in the promises of God is a hope that will not disappoint. All other hope is fragile: "What he trusts in is fragile; what he relies on is a spider's web. He leans on his web, but it gives way; he clings to it, but it does not hold" (Job 8:14-15).

Suffering

"And we rejoice in the hope of the glory of God. Not only so, but we also rejoice in our sufferings, because we know that suffering produces perseverance; perseverance, character; and character, hope. And hope does not disappoint us, because God has poured out his love into our hearts by the Holy Spirit, whom he has given us" (Rom. 5:2-5).

The following list itemizes some things people put their hope in. Look through the list. If the hope is a "fragile hope" (a hope that can disappoint), put an "x" in the box in front of it.

❑ Beauty and reputation (Ezek. 16:15)
❑ Neighbors and friends (Mic. 7:5)
❑ Physical safety and comfort (Deut. 28:52)
❑ Relatives (Jer. 9:4)
❑ Health and strength (Jer. 17:5)
❑ Wealth and possessions (Prov. 11:28)
❑ Might and power (Isa. 31:3)

❑ False gods and idols (Jer. 13:25)
❑ Personal competence (Isa. 2:22)
❑ Self (Hab. 2:18)
❑ Long life (Isa. 2:22)
❑ Leaders and other people (Ps. 146:3)
❑ Favorable circumstances (Ps. 112:7)
❑ Desires being fulfilled (Ps. 112:10)

Have you leaned on any of these hopes and found that, like a spider's web, they've given way? Circle the ones that have disappointed you.

In our culture, *hope* basically means "wishful thinking." Unfortunately, we often place our hope in that which is fragile. Did you mark all the boxes in the exercise above? All of these hopes can disappoint.

The biblical concept of hope involves certainty. Biblical hope is joyful and confident expectation that God will fulfill His promises. Biblical hope gives me the rock-solid assurance that a time will come when there will be no more pain, or sorrow, or weeping. He will wipe every tear from our eyes!

Read Hebrews 6:18-19 in the margin. How does verse 19 describe hope

in God? _____

Hebrews probably was written to the believers in Rome facing trials and difficulties. Many were discouraged. Their hope of an easy ride in life had given way. But those who "fled to take hold of the hope" of God were greatly encouraged. God's hope is an "anchor for the soul, firm and secure."

Where are you placing your hope? Think about a stress or difficulty you are currently facing. Are you holding on to spider webs or to the anchor?
❑ spider webs ❑ anchor ❑ a bit of both ❑ I'm not sure.

"God did this so that, by two unchangeable things in which it is impossible for God to lie, we who have fled to take hold of the hope offered to us may be greatly encouraged. We have this hope as an anchor for the soul, firm and secure" (Heb. 6:18-19).

Holding God's anchor at times feels like blind trust. How can we put our faith in that which we cannot see? Read today's Climbing Gear to learn more about climbing blind.

Blind Trust

Erik Weihenmayer was the first blind person to climb to the top of the highest peak on each of the seven continents. To make it to the top, Erik had to listen carefully to the little bell tied to the back of the climber in front of him so he would know which way to go. He also needed to listen to the instructions of his guide. On Everest, they were fitted with special throat microphones and ear plugs so they could communicate in spite of oxygen masks. According to Eric, the greatest fear in climbing blind is in the reaching. To climb higher, he needs to trust his guide, let go of his secure perch, and reach for what he cannot see. His level of success is directly related to his level of trust.

We are all climbing blind. We "see but a poor reflection" of the future that is in store (1 Cor. 13:12). But we achieve success by fixing our eyes on the invisible (2 Cor. 4:16-18). In times of difficulty, we need to reach out and grab hold of the unseen hope. It's in trusting our guide, Jesus, that we make it to the top.

"He gives strength to the weary and increases the power of the weak. Even youths grow tired and weary, and young men stumble and fall; but those who hope in the LORD will renew their strength. They will soar on wings like eagles; they will run and not grow weary, they will walk and not be faint" (Isa. 40: 29-31).

It's not easy to keep cycling when the hills are steep. But the feeling of victory riding into Banff after five

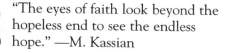

"The eyes of faith look beyond the hopeless end to see the endless hope." —M. Kassian

days of struggle is unbelievable. On the road of life, Jesus has promised to be our help, our guide, and our hiding place. He has promised to lead us from "strength to strength" until we appear before the Lord in Zion (Ps. 84:7). And on that day, the joy of victory will be unbelievable! To finish this week's study, read Isaiah 40: 29-31 in the margin. Pray, asking the Lord to help you fix your hope on Him.

Vertically Inclined

The Mount of Affection
Godward Climbers Keep Their Love Alive

af•fec•tion—the inclinations, longings, compulsions that move us towards the object of our desire. Devotion; love; tenderness; a fond feeling of attachment to another.

Base Camp
From the freezing cold of the Columbia Glacial Icefields to the steaming mineral water of Banff Hot Springs … in this week's base camp we'll go from one extreme to the other to learn more about what it takes to keep love alive. According to John, "the disciple whom Jesus loved" (John 13:23), it IS possible to have an affection that grows hotter with the passing of time!

Daily Lessons
Day 1: Higher Levels of Love
     … Seized by Affection
Day 2: Higher Levels of Devotion
     … Compelled by Affection
Day 3: Higher Levels of Compassion
     … Moved by Affection
Day 4: Higher Levels of Tenderness
     … Softened by Affection
Day 5: Higher Levels of Endearment
     … Sustained by Affection

High Points
- Hills of Nazareth
- Mount Hermon
- Mount Samaria
- Mount Gilead
- Mount Lebanon

Climbing Gear
- Triumph Over Tit-for-Tat
- Growth Chart

Memory Pack
"We know and rely on the love God has for us. God is love. Whoever lives in love lives in God, and God in him" (1 John 4:16).

The Mount of Affection: Seized by a Great Affection
I John 4:7-21

Summit 5—

The Mount of Affection

This Base Camp Guide will help you follow the video session for Summit 5.

Affections, the inclinations, longings, compulsions that move us toward the object of our desire.

1. Power to Seize Your Affections

a. He is the _____ _____. (v. 7-8—"God is love")

b. Affection _____ affection. (v. 9-10—"live through him")

c. Those who have been seized _____ it! (v. 13,16—"we know")

2. Power to Transform Your Affections

a. Transforms core _____ (v. 18—"no fear")
   • _____ of righteousness instead of _____ of punishment

b. Transforms core _____ (v. 17—"like him")

c. Transforms core _____ (v. 19-21—"love his brother")

3. Power to Sustain Your Affections

a. Affection that _____ (v. 15-16—"know and rely")
   • a consuming fire (Heb. 12:29)

b. Affection that _____ (v. 17-18—"made complete")
   • increases in knowledge and depth of insight (Phil. 1:9)

c. Affection that _____ (v. 14—"seen and testify")
   • "_____ _____" behavior (Rev. 2:4-5)

d. Affection that _____ (v. 17—"confidence")

Do you feel your desire growing cold? Remember your "first love." Push deeper into the burning heart of Christ. That's the way to conquer the Mount of Affection.

DAY 1

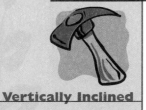

Vertically Inclined

Higher Levels of Love ...

Seized by Affection

In the 1730s and 1740s, New England and other colonies along the Eastern seaboard experienced a religious revival that has come to be known as the Great Awakening. During that time, people who became followers of Jesus had a unique expression for their salvation experience. They'd say, "I've been seized by the power of a great affection!"

God fervently and unrelentingly pursues a relationship with us. The New Englanders "seized" by His affection responded with a fervor of their own. God's affection stirred their affections, and they became passionate about pursuing God.

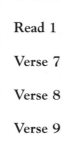

"One loving heart sets another on fire."—Isaac Watts[1]

One of the central figures in the Great Awakening was a minister of a church in Northampton, Massachusetts, named Jonathan Edwards. His church was one of the epicenters for the revival. Edwards witnessed hundreds of conversions. He watched as the spiritual fervor escalated. Then he watched that fervor cool off. Many who had demonstrated what appeared to be genuine spiritual zeal lost their excitement and became indifferent. After the revival passed, Edwards wrote a book entitled, *The Religious Affections*. In it, he explored the question of what it takes to have an affection that lasts and grows, and does not diminish over time.

This week we'll learn more about affection, because every Godward climber needs to know how to keep the fires of love burning.

Understanding the Basics (Loving God 101)

According to the dictionary, to *love* is to "have a strong liking for or to take great pleasure in." It's a feeling of interest, attraction, and attachment. How do we begin to love God? How do we develop a strong liking for Him?

Read 1 John 4:7-10,19. What do these verses teach us about loving God?

Verse 7: _____

Verse 8: _____

Verse 9: _____

Verse 10: _____

98   Verse 19: _____

In 1 John this beloved disciple instructs us on the Christian meaning of love. He teaches that love is not a human achievement, but rather a gift that is divine in origin: "Love comes from God" (1 John 4:7). We will never understand love if we think it starts from the human end. John maintains that to see what love really means we must see ourselves as sinners, deserving of God's wrath, and yet as those for whom He sacrificed His only Son. Apart from God we cannot love God. It's impossible. We cannot initiate affection. We can only respond to His great affection: "We love because he first loved us" (1 John 4:19).

Look up the following verses and match each reference with the thought it presents.

Romans 5:5

Romans 8:15-16

Ephesians 3:16-17

Galatians 5:22

God has poured His love into our hearts by the Holy Spirit.

The Spirit "roots" and "establishes" us in love.

Love is a fruit of the Spirit dwelling in our hearts.

The Spirit fills us with a longing for our heavenly Father.

God gives us the ability to love. He puts His Spirit—the Spirit of love—into our hearts. It's like a mother helping her very young child color a picture. The mother suggests the idea, prepares a space at the table, provides a coloring book and crayons, and shows the child how to color inside the lines. Mom provides the direction and resources. The child merely cooperates.

Read Acts 2:38 in the margin. Circle the picture that best represents the process whereby our hearts are filled with love for God.

Love is a gift we receive when we receive the gift of the Holy Spirit. God's love for us is a gift. Our love for Him is also a gift. God gives us this gift when we put our faith in Jesus Christ for the forgiveness of sins.

Every morning and evening, Jews recited the Shema (Heb. "hear"), the classic Jewish declaration of faith: "Hear, O Israel: The LORD our God, the

Summit 5—
The Mount of Affection

"Peter replied, 'Repent and be baptized, every one of you, in the name of Jesus Christ for the forgiveness of your sins. And you will receive the gift of the Holy Spirit' " (Acts 2:38).

LORD is one. Love the LORD your God with all your heart and with all your soul and with all your strength" (Deut. 6:4-5). Devout Jews wore the verses on slips of parchment strapped to their heads and/or arms in small boxes called phylacteries. They also kept a copy in their mezuzahs—containers affixed to the doorpost of their homes (Deut. 4:8-9).

No Jews were more devout than the Pharisees. They were known for their detailed interpretation of the minute aspects of the law (Matt. 9:14; 23:15; Luke 11:39; 18:12). They were fastidious about obeying the commandments. The Pharisees prided themselves in being the best at applying the Shema. They made "their phylacteries wide and the tassels on their garments long" so everyone would notice how much they loved God (Matt. 23:5).

The Pharisees were so self-righteous that they were offended when Jesus taught that loving God meant loving and accepting Jesus as the Son of God (John 5:39-42). According to Jesus, it was presumptuous for the Pharisees to think that they could love God through human effort. Ironically, it was their pride in their own ability to love God that kept the Pharisees from truly loving Him. When Jesus confronted their hypocrisy, their hearts were filled with condemnation and hatred toward Him. So much so, that they plotted to kill Jesus at the first available opportunity.

Read today's High Point to find out about a mob attempt on Jesus' life in His hometown—in the hills of Nazareth.

Read 1 John 4:10,15-16. The Pharisees and Jews in Nazareth believed they loved God. In the margin, explain why they were mistaken.

Hatred in the Hometown: Hills of Nazareth
Jesus grew up in Nazareth, a small agricultural village along the southern ridge of the Lebanon range. The town was situated about 14 miles from the Sea of Galilee and about 6 miles west of Mount Tabor. During Jesus' time, it appears to have had a population of less than 2,000 persons.

Nazareth was built on a high valley surrounded on three sides by steep limestone hills. To the south there was a sharp drop to the Plain of Esdraelon. Because it was in the foot of the mountains, there were plenty of jagged rocks and cliffs in and around the town. It was from one such jutting prominence that a mob tried to throw Jesus down, headlong, in order to kill him.

What had He done to incite such anger? It was His hometown after all—the place He had lived for almost 30 years. In the 2 or 3 short years since His departure He had gained a sizable reputation for His teaching skills. Rumor had it He also performed astonishing miracles. Now He had returned, and the synagogue in Nazareth was buzzing with anticipation. Pharisees, religious

"This is love: not that we loved God, but that he loved us and sent his Son as an atoning sacrifice for our sins. ... If anyone acknowledges that Jesus is the Son of God, God lives in him and he in God. And so we know and rely on the love God has for us"
(1 John 4:10, 15-16)

leaders, and common folk were all curiously fascinated with the one whom they had known only as the carpenter's boy. What would He say? One can just imagine the "C'mon, Jesus, impress us!" attitude that permeated the room.

Jesus unrolled the scroll and read Isaiah's prophetic words about the Messiah. They were duly impressed with His oratory skills. Then he said, "Today this scripture is fulfilled in your hearing" (Luke 4:21).

"Who does this guy think he is?" the crowd began to murmur. "Didn't he grow up down the street?" Jesus sensed their pride and growing opposition. He knew what they were thinking.

Jesus warned them that when the Jews had previously rejected God's love, God had bypassed them and offered His blessing to individuals outside the nation of Israel. The implication was that if they rejected Jesus as Messiah, God would bypass them and extend His love to others.

The crowd in the synagogue exploded in fury. How audacious of Jesus to suggest that loving God meant believing in Jesus. How dare He question their love? In anger they mobbed Him and dragged Him to the brow of the cliff to throw Him off. But Jesus escaped. The Messiah was destined to give His life on a cross, not on the cliff at Nazareth (Luke 4:14-30).

> "On the whole, God's love for us is a much safer subject to think about than our love for Him."
> —C.S. Lewis[2]

Know and Rely

The Pharisees and Jews in Nazareth didn't understand what it meant to love God. That's because they self-righteously thought they could love Him on their terms and in their own strength. Based on today's lesson, we can summarize the following truths about love.

1. Apart from God we cannot love. Love starts with Him.
2. God is love. He alone defines the true meaning of love.
3. True love is discerned in the person and sacrifice of Jesus.
4. Love is a gift we receive when we receive the gift of the Holy Spirit.
5. We must depend on God to understand love and grow in love.

To close today's lesson, reread 1 John 4:10,15-16 in the margin on page 100. Circle the words *know* and *rely*. Ask the Lord to help you know and rely on His love.

Higher Levels of Devotion ...
Compelled by Affection

Vertically Inclined

"And this is love: that we walk in obedience to his commands. As you have heard from the beginning, his command is that you walk in love" (2 John 6).

Which came first—the chicken or the egg? I just did an Internet search and am amazed at the dozens of Web sites that are devoted to the question. The self-proclaimed "smartest man in America" argues that evolutionary mutations occur in reproductive rather than somatic DNA, and thus, the egg came first. Many Christians disagree. They say that since God created the fowl of the air, and no mention is made of Him creating eggs, the chicken came first. Other Christians maintain that chickens, like most of our domesticated animals, came about by interbreeding. God created wild fowl, not domesticated ones, hence, the egg came first.

First thing this morning, as we were getting out of bed, I posed the question to my husband. "I'm thinking about a classic question, and I'd like your opinion. Which came first—the chicken or the egg?"

Brent looked at me for a long moment and retorted, "Coffee came first and I'm going downstairs to make some!" His answer is as good as any. Whether the chicken or the egg came first is inconsequential. All we know for certain is that the chicken comes from the egg, and the egg comes from the chicken, and God is responsible for putting the whole process into place.

"Wicked men obey from fear, good men, from love."
—Aristotle[3]

A Chicken and Egg Scenario
Use the verse in the margin to complete the following sentences:

Love for God is: _____

His command is: _____

Look up the Scriptures and fill in the blanks that follow.

John 15:10   We remain in God's love by _____ His commands.

John 14:15   If we love Jesus, we will _____ His commands.

1 John 3:23   God's command is to _____ in Jesus and to _____ one another.

Mark 12:29-30   The most important command is to _____ God.

Love leads to obedience, which leads to love. One flows from the other in such a circular manner it's virtually impossible to discern which comes first, or where one ends and the other begins. In our relationship with God, love and obedience define each other. The Bible teaches that love without obedience isn't really love, and that obedience without love isn't really obedience.

The Bible gives examples of those who appeared obedient but were lacking in love, as well as those who appeared to love, but were lacking in obedience. Look up the verses below. If the individuals were lacking love, cross out the heart, and if they were lacking obedience, cross out the tablets.

As we discussed yesterday, the Pharisees were fastidious about obeying the minutest details of the Mosaic Law. They were "doers" who prided themselves in obedience. But obedience without love results in self-righteous legalism. The people of Judah were highly demonstrative in their worship. They were "feelers." To express their devotion, they offered God expensive, exotic incense imported from Sheba, and sweet calamus, an aromatic rue, which came from India. They appeared to have a deep love for the Lord, but were lacking in obedience. God's charge against them was that though they worshiped with passion, they continued to do as they pleased (Isa. 58:3,13). Love without obedience merely results in self-indulgent emotionalism.

Love and obedience are indivisibly related. To love we need to obey. To obey we need to love. Jesus' post-resurrection question to Peter: "Do you love me?" reflects this (John 21:16,17). The first two times Jesus asked the question, He used the word *agapan* for love. The third time, he used the word *philein*. *Agapan* has more to do with a volitional and deliberate intellectual choice (doing), whereas *philein* has more to do with a deeply felt, emotional attachment (feeling).[4] In John, these two words are used interchangeably. That's because true love involves both. Affection for God involves a deeply felt, emotional attachment as well as a deliberate intellectual choice.

Many people in the church are imbalanced in their affection for God. They focus on feeling or doing to the exclusion of the other. Those who pride themselves in doing (obedience) tend to be critical of those who struggle with sin. Their hearts are callous, with a "Why can't those other people just pull up their socks?" attitude—and they are emotionally unmoved in worship. On the other extreme, those who pride themselves in feeling worship God with emotional fervor; yet do not take sin seriously. They are casual about dealing with sins such as lust, adultery, slander, envy, impatience, resentment, deceit, and insubordination. Both the feeler and doer are filled with a sense of pride. Both believe they are doing a good job of loving God.

Put an "X" on the scale to indicate your tendency toward legalism or emotionalism.

Self-righteous legalism   Loyal love   Self-centered emotionalism

I have been on both sides of the spectrum; though I tend toward legalism. Maintaining both wholehearted passion AND wholehearted obedience requires a great deal of humility. It requires an attitude of dependence. I need God's help to love Him loyally. I cannot do it on my own.

If You Please

Over the years, I've received some unusual gifts from my husband. One Christmas, I received a cordless power drill. Another, I received a bike seat (anatomically designed for females). You may laugh, but Brent's gifts indicate that he is well aware of what pleases me. I was very pleased with the power drill and bike seat. They were just what I wanted.

When we love someone, we want to please that person. Brent wants to know and do what pleases me and I want to know and do what pleases him. "Seeking to please" demonstrates love and helps love grow. It involves getting to know the individual—his or her personality, likes, and dislikes— and doing what brings that person joy.

Pleasing God is how we demonstrate our love for Him. That's why there's such a close link between love and obedience. Obeying God is simply knowing and doing what pleases Him.

In Ephesians 5:10, what did Paul recommend to keep love for Christ growing? _____

In the margin, brainstorm things you think please God. (If you'd like help, refer to Ps. 19:14; Prov. 15:8-9; Rom. 12:1; 14:17-18; Eph. 5:8-11; Col. 1:10.) Read more about pleasing God in today's High Point.

Pleasing God: Mount Hermon

Looking north from virtually anywhere in Palestine one can see the pale, blue, snow-capped peaks of Mount Hermon (Heb., sacred), marking the northern boundary of the promised land (Deut. 3:8; 4:48; Josh. 11:3). Mount Hermon is about 40 miles north of the Sea of Galilee. It's the most conspicuous mountain in the region, accounting for it's modern name of Jebel-esh-Sheikh, "the chief mountain."

Mount Hermon receives heavy precipitation on its summit and western slopes—over 40 inches each year. This filters down through the porous sandstone to become the source of the Jordan and Litani rivers and the oasis of Damascus. In antiquity, the mountain was thickly forested, and abundant in vineyards and orchards.

Mount Hermon has three summits. The city of Caesarea Philippi is located at its base. Many believe it is the "high mountain" Jesus and His disciples—Peter, James, and John—climbed to spend a night in prayer (Mark 8:27). As He was praying that night, Jesus was transfigured before them. "His face shone like the sun, and his clothes became as white as the light (Matt. 17:2). Then, a booming voice announced from heaven, "This is my Son, whom I love; with him I am well pleased" (Matt. 17:5).

The Greek word *transfigure* is the same as our English word *metamorphosis*. It means "a change from within." Jesus allowed His inner glory to be revealed to the disciples. His inner glory transformed His external appearance. The same word is used in Romans 12:1-2, "Offer your bodies as living sacrifices, holy and pleasing to God … be transformed [transfigured] by the renewing of your mind." Pursuing holiness transforms us to become more and more like Jesus. This is how we please God and demonstrate our love for Him.

"I will give you a new heart and put a new spirit in you; I will remove from you your heart of stone and give you a heart of flesh. And I will put my Spirit in you and move you to follow my decrees and be careful to keep my laws" (Ezek. 36:26-27).

"Obedience to God is the most infallible evidence of sincere and supreme love to him."
—Nathanael Emmons[5]

To close today, consider how you might please God. Do you need to be more obedient? Does your heart need to be reignited with love? Read Ezekiel 36:26-27 in the margin. Ask the Lord to soften your heart and help you obey His Word. Take a moment to listen. Is there something the Lord wants you to do in response to what you learned today?

Higher Levels of Compassion ...

Moved by Affection

To check the chlorine levels of our hot tub, I dip a small test strip into the water. The chlorine in the water reacts with the chemicals on the test strip, changing the color of the test patch from white to purple. The deeper the color, the higher the level of chlorine. The test is visible proof of the "invisible" condition of the water. Without it, it would be very difficult to determine how much chlorine the water contains.

According to 1 John 4:19-21, what's the "litmus test" to determine the extent to which our hearts are filled with love for God?

- ❑ How long and how often we pray
- ❑ How regularly we go to church
- ❑ How passionately we worship
- ❑ How careful we are to complete our Bible studies
- ❑ How much we love those around us
- ❑ How much money we donate

Loving God and loving people are the "flesh and skin" of love. They are so indivisibly related that you can't have one without the other. The litmus test of our love for God is our love for those around us.

The " 'first and greatest commandment' " is to love God. A closely related second commandment is to " 'love your neighbor as yourself' " (Matt. 22:37-40). The two are so closely related that in Romans 13:9, Paul is able to say that all the commands can be summed up in the rule, "Love your neighbor as yourself." The command to love your neighbor as yourself is "the royal law" (Jas. 2:8).

Explain in the margin what you think it means to "love your neighbor as yourself."

Neighbor to Neighbor

One day a Jewish expert in the law approached Jesus with a question, "What must I do to inherit eternal life?" (Luke 10:25). It was a sly question. He was secretly trying to get Jesus into trouble. He knew people were saying that Jesus was the Messiah—the One through whom deliverance was promised. He also knew Jesus claimed to be "the way" to the Father (John. 14:6).

" 'What is written in the law?' " [Jesus] replied, " 'How do you read it?' " The expert cited the Shema: "Love the Lord your God with all your heart and with all your soul and with all your strength and with all your mind, and love your neighbor as yourself." " 'You have answered correctly,' " Jesus replied.

Not satisfied, the expert tried to goad Him with what he thought was another extremely clever question: "Who is my neighbor?"

The expert wanted Jesus to acknowledge His righteousness. Instead, he told a parable about a Jewish man traveling from Jerusalem to Jericho. Along the way, the man was ambushed and beaten by a band of robbers who left him, half dead, on the road. A Jewish priest and a Levite (also a Jew) passed by the crumpled body but refused to get involved. Finally, a Samaritan stopped. He took the man for medical treatment, and paid for all the expenses.

"Which of these three do you think was a neighbor to the man who fell into the hands of robbers?" Jesus asked.

The expert was trapped. By definition, the only people Jews considered "neighbors" were fellow Jews. Jews and Samaritans hated one another. Yet in Christ's parable, the neighbors of the injured Jew didn't act very neighborly. The Samaritan—the Jew's archenemy and rival—was the only one who demonstrated compassion.

Who was the injured man's neighbor? The expert took a big gulp. (He couldn't force himself to say the Samaritan.) "I suppose it was the one who had mercy on him," he stammered. Jesus turned the tables. The expert in the law prided himself in how much he loved his neighbor. But Jesus exposed the hatred hidden in his heart. Can you imagine the embarrassment and anger as the challenger slithered away (Luke 10:25-37)?

According to this parable, who's your neighbor? Check all that apply.

❏ **People that live next door**
❏ **Colleagues at work**
❏ **Players on the competing team**
❏ **The salesclerk at the store**
❏ **Friends at church**
❏ **People who hate and mistreat me**
❏ **The guy who cut me off in traffic**
❏ **My family (in-laws and exes included)**

According to Jesus, *neighbor* isn't restricted to those who live close to you or to those who treat you well. Neighbor includes everyone—even those who hate you. Did you check all the boxes? The royal law requires that we love our enemies. Read today's High Point on Mount Samaria to find out why the Jews were enemies with their neighbors, the Samaritans.

Enemies as Neighbors: Mount Samaria

When the promised land was divided up, the descendants of Joseph's two sons, Manasseh and Ephraim, were allotted the central hill country north and south of the twin mountains:

Gerizim and Ebal. Just a few miles west of these mountains stands a big, oblong hill with a long, flat top—the hill of "Shomeron," (Samaria) which means observer or watchtower. The hill is steep on three sides, rising about 300 feet above the surrounding valleys, but has a long, sloping ridge to the east. It was the ideal site for a fortified city. Omri, king of the northern kingdom of Israel, purchased the hill for two talents of silver, and built his residence on its broad summit (1 Kings 16:24). The city of Samaria remained the capital of Israel until the time of the Assyrian conquest (2 Kings 7:1-20; 17:3; 18:9-12). At that time, the King of Assyria exiled vast numbers of Israelites to Babylon. To repopulate and assimilate the region, he ordered Babylonian citizens to relocate to Samaria. The new inhabitants amalgamated with the remaining Jews, creating a population of Jewish-Gentile half-breeds—"Samaritans."

After the exile, Jews returned to Jerusalem to rebuild the temple. The Samaritans offered to help, but were spurned because of their mixed ancestry. Offended, they built a rival temple on Mount Gerizim. The Jews believed this was sacrilege. Hostilities between the two groups erupted. In 128 B.C., a Jewish king razed the temple on Gerizim to the ground. The Samaritans rebuilt it in Shechem, a city on Gerizim's lower slopes. The enmity escalated. During a passover in about A.D. 7, some Samaritans desecrated the temple in Jerusalem by scattering human bones on the floor. The hatred between the two groups was fierce and well entrenched. The Jews used the term "Samaritan" as one of bitter contempt and avoided all dealings with them (John. 4:9; 8:48). Bloody confrontations between Jews and Samaritans were not uncommon.

Jesus recognized the Samaritans weren't Jews, yet He didn't treat them as other Jews did. Jesus rebuked His disciples for their hatred (Luke 9:55). He freely interacted with the Samaritan woman (John 4:7) and the Samaritan leper (Luke 17:16). When the pious, Jewish expert in the law questioned Jesus on how to love one's neighbor, Jesus used the illustration of a Samaritan caring for a Jew. True love treats enemies as friends. Loving your neighbor means having compassion on those who hate you.

"They love indeed who quake to say they love."—Philip Sidney[6]

"Neighborliness" Report Card

Think of a person with whom you've had unpleasant interaction. Jot down that person's first or last initial: _____. According to Jesus, that person is your neighbor. How loving are you toward him or her?

Read Luke 6:27-38. Then fill out the following report card. Each description presents the biblical ideal of a loving "neighbor." Based

on your relationship with the person you identified above, how do you compare? Give yourself a "grade" in the space beside each point. (A) Excellent (B) Above Average (C) Average (D) Below Average (F) Failure.

GRADE	Act of "Neighborliness"
_____	1. I have a charitable disposition toward my neighbor. I am friendly and not antagonistic.
_____	2. My favorable attitude is backed up by the kindness of my deeds. I look for opportunities to do good for my neighbor.
_____	3. My words are gracious. I do not let any unwholesome talk come out of my mouth but only what is helpful for building my neighbor up.
_____	4. I pray regularly for my neighbor. The more difficult our relationship, the more earnestly I pray.
_____	5. I do not retaliate when my neighbor treats me poorly. I am open and not defensive. I do not seek revenge.
_____	6. I am willing to give above and beyond what my neighbor gives. I do not keep a tally of who has contributed more to the relationship.
_____	7. I do not focus on my rights, but on my responsibility. I have no expectations of my neighbor. I love with "no strings attached."
_____	8. I am merciful. I treat my neighbor much better than he or she "deserves." I show mercy in proportion to the mercy God has shown me.
_____	9. I do not judge and condemn my neighbor. I do not curse and/or wish evil upon him or her. I leave justice to God.
_____	10. I forgive. I do not hold a grudge. I keep my spirit free from bitterness and anger. I forgive in proportion to how much God has forgiven me.

The person I currently have a difficult time loving is someone who has betrayed, defrauded, and slandered my husband. It's very sobering for me to consider that my love for this person is an indicator of my love for God. How desperately I need God to intervene in my heart and help me love mercifully, as Jesus loved! We'll be learning more about that tomorrow. But today I'd like you to finish up by asking God to help you love your "neighbor." Listen to what the Holy Spirit says to you. Jot your thoughts in the margin.

DAY 4

Higher Levels of Tenderness ...

Softened by Affection

Vertically Inclined

Tit-for-Tat is the name of a Laurel and Hardy slapstick comedy released in 1935. In the film, Stan and Ollie open a hardware shop right next to Charlie Hall's grocery store. A misunderstanding occurs and Hall takes revenge on Stan and Ollie. Stan and Ollie retaliate. The back-and-forth antics start with silly attacks such as mashed potatoes in the face, eggs cracked on the head, a curling iron pressed on the nose, and escalate in intensity until both the hardware shop and grocery store are on the verge of being demolished. Thankfully, Officer James C. Morton intervenes, helps the parties reconcile, and restores the peace.

The phrase, "tit-for-tat" dates back to the 16th century. *Tit* is an old Middle English word meaning "tug" or "jerk." *Tat* comes from the Middle English *tatelen* meaning to prattle or tattle. The phrase refers to an exchange of insults or attacks involving retribution or retaliation. It's based on an ancient law that dates back to the time of the patriarchs.

The British say "tit for tat," the Dutch—"dit vor dat," and the French— "tant pour tant." Look up Leviticus 24:19-20. Write out the corresponding ancient Hebrew phrases.

_____

Exodus 21:24-25 includes other examples: hand for hand, foot for foot, burn for burn, wound for wound, and bruise for bruise. These verses are part of the *lex talionis*: the law of retaliation, which was widespread throughout the Near East. It was a judicial principle that ensured that the punishment fit the crime. It protected the innocent by ensuring that justice was served, but also protected the guilty by ensuring that the punishment was not overly excessive. If a man poked out his neighbor's eye, the eye of the offender would be the maximum penalty the neighbor could demand.

Using the lex talionis law of justice, determine the fair and just payment for the following "crimes." Write the judgment in the space to the left of each crime. The first one is done for you.

_____**Life**_____ for life	_____ for slander
_____ for money	_____ for deceit
_____ for sarcasm	_____ for criticism

110

Do you ever administer judgment according to the lex talionis law (for example, screaming at someone who screamed at you)?
❑ never ❑ seldom ❑ sometimes ❑ often ❑ almost always

The lex talionis law of justice is one that's deeply ingrained in the human spirit. Just think of the cries of two feuding children. The "She hit me!" is almost inevitably followed by the defense, "He hit me first!" When someone injures us, we feel justified in injuring that person in return. In order to serve justice, we want to administer a "tit for tat" judgment on their crime.

The lex talionis law governed fair and just judgment, but there were additional concepts that God's people were to take into consideration when deciding how to act toward an offender: mercy, compassion, and humility. "This is what the LORD Almighty says: 'Administer true justice; show mercy and compassion to one another'" (Zech. 7:9). "And what does the LORD require of you? To act justly and to love mercy and to walk humbly with your God" (Mic. 6:8).

Certain cities in Israel were designated as "cities of refuge"—places where offenders could find mercy. Read more about it in today's High Point.

> "Being all fashioned of self-same dust, Let us be merciful as well as just." —Henry Wadsworth Longfellow[7]

Mercy Me: Mount Gilead

The law dictated that to keep the land of Israel holy, the shed blood of an innocent person needed to be avenged—life for life (Num. 35:33). In the Mosaic penal code, it was the right and duty of the nearest relative of a murdered person to slay the murderer. The relative was called the "avenger" or "redeemer" of blood (Num. 35:27). So this law would not be abused, Moses appointed six Levitical cities throughout Israel as cities of refuge, where the offender could flee and present his case to the priestly authorities. (Ex. 21:13; Deut. 19:1-2,9). If he was found innocent of deliberately premeditating the murder, he was extended mercy and given sanctuary in the city.

Ramoth-gilead was one of the cities of refuge. It was situated along a major trade route, "the King's Highway," in the mountainous province of Gilead. *Ramoth* means "a broad height," while *Gilead* means "hill of testimony." This indicates that it was a fortified city built on a hill. Gilead was a richly wooded area famous for its healing balm. A type of balsam tree, unique to the area, yielded a highly valued medicinal balm that was exported to Egypt and Tyre (Gen. 37:25; Jer. 8:22; 46:11; Ezek. 27:17).

According to legend, King Solomon originally received these trees as a gift from the Queen of Sheba (1 Kings 10:10).

"Is there no balm in Gilead. Is there no physician there?" the prophet Jeremiah lamented (Jer. 8:22). It was a rhetorical question. Gilead was a place of abundant mercy and healing. The prophet obviously knew that. But he was at a loss to understand why the Israelites would choose to incur God's judgment rather than running to Him for refuge to find mercy.

Mercy Triumphs Over Judgment

God's mercy and compassion have always tempered His judgment. But the full extent of His mercy wasn't revealed until He sent His one and only Son to die for us. According to the law, eternal death is what we deserve. But because of God's great mercy, we are offered eternal life. This offer became possible through Jesus, who "fulfilled" all the demands of the law (Matt. 5:17-18). All fair and just penalties—eye for eye, tooth for tooth, and life for life—were paid on the cross with His holy blood. That's why we who believe in Jesus are no longer "under" the letter of the law. We are free to live by a greater standard—one that more closely mirrors God's compassion.

Read the passages in the margin on this page and page 113. In each, circle the phrase "but I tell you." Jesus was comparing the letter of the old covenant to the heart of the new. "This is what the letter of the law says, BUT I tell you …" Underline the reasons Jesus gave for this radical behavior.

Children of God act like their Father. They follow God's example of extending mercy to those who least deserve it. Instead of demanding justice, they treat others as God has treated them. In the passages you just read, did you underline the reasons: "that you may be sons of your Father in heaven," and "just as your Father is merciful"?

Read the parable about the unmerciful servant in Matthew 18:21-35. What does this parable teach about judgment and mercy?

_____

Which would you rather receive: ❑ God's judgment or ❑ His mercy?

How do you normally respond to those who mistreat you? Put an "x" on the scale at the top of the next page to indicate your normal response.

Vertically Inclined

" 'You have heard that it was said, "Eye for eye, and tooth for tooth." But I tell you, Do not resist an evil person. If someone strikes you on the right cheek, turn to him the other also. … If someone forces you to go one mile, go with him two miles. Give to the one who asks you, and do not turn away from the one who wants to borrow from you' " (Matt. 5:38-39,41-42).

" 'You have heard that it was said, "Love your neighbor and hate your enemy." But I tell you: Love your enemies and pray for those who persecute you, that you may be sons of your Father in heaven' " (Matt. 5:43-44).

**I respond with
tit-for-tat judgment.**

**I respond with
great mercy.**

James 2:13 contains a warning as well as a promise. First, it says, "judgment without mercy will be shown to anyone who has not been merciful." Read those words slowly and let the meaning sink in: "Judgment without mercy will be shown to anyone who has not been merciful."

I don't know about you, but that warning strikes fear in my heart. I "judge" others whenever I treat them according to what I feel they "deserve," rather than according to the mercy God has shown me. I need only think of how impatient I was with the girl who served me so slowly at the coffee shop this morning to see that I am guilty of judging. The thought makes me fall to my knees in shame and beg God for mercy. And that leads me to the second part of James 2:13, the promise: "Mercy triumphs over judgment!" The word *triumphs* is a unique word that means, "to be superior; to boast in triumphant comparison with." Because of Jesus, God's mercy takes priority over His judgment. Thus, He doesn't condemn me for my lack of mercy. Realizing this makes me love Him all the more. And loving Him compels me to love my neighbor by extending more mercy.

Take a moment to thank God for His great mercy. Ask Him to give you a merciful heart. Put on today's Climbing Gear to help you triumph over tit-for-tat judgment.

" 'But I tell you who hear me: Love your enemies, do good to those who hate you, bless those who curse you, pray for those who mistreat you. … Be merciful, just as your Father is merciful' "
(Luke 6:27-28,36).

"A part of kindness consists in loving people more than they deserve." —Joseph Joubert[8]

Triumph Over
Tit-for-Tat

By nature, we want to return insult for insult, anger for anger, slander for slander, betrayal for betrayal, bruise for bruise, and wound for wound. But whenever we treat someone tit-for-tat as we believe they "deserve" rather than treating them according to the mercy God has shown us, we are guilty of judging. Christ can set you free from this habit. As you depend on Him, He will empower you to respond to evil with good. The next time someone offends you, make a conscious decision to avoid tit-for-tat. Focus on God's mercy. Treat the offender with the same kindness God has extended to you.

113

Higher Levels of Endearment ...

Sustained by Affection

Vertically Inclined

7 *"The righteous will flourish like a palm tree, they will grow like a cedar of Lebanon; planted in the house of the Lord, they will flourish in the courts of our God. They will still bear fruit in old age, they will stay fresh and green"* (Ps. 92:12-14).

The question we're addressing this week is how to keep our love for God alive and growing. It's an important question. In Matthew 24:12 Jesus predicted, "… the love of most will grow cold." Jonathan Edwards saw that happen after the Great Awakening. I've seen it happen, and I'm sure you have, too. How do we sustain a burning love for God?

Here's a summary of what we've learned so far:

Day 1: Growing in love means growing in **humble dependence.** God is love. Love's expression is centered in the cross. We are desperately dependent upon Christ to understand love and grow in love.

Day 2: Growing in love means growing in **obedience.** Love and obedience are indivisibly linked. Love without obedience isn't really love—obedience without love isn't really obedience.

Day 3: Growing in love means growing in **neighborliness.** The more we love God, the more radically we will love our enemies. If we don't love them, we don't really love Him.

Day 4: Growing in love means growing in **mercy.** The more we love God, the more merciful we will be. We will not treat others according to what we feel they deserve, but rather according to the mercy God has shown us.

We could add more points to the list. Growing in love also means growing in self-sacrifice, commitment, generosity, peace, knowledge, insight, and more. But, the bottom line is in order to keep our love for God growing, *we* need to keep growing.

Our love for God grows as we grow to be more like Jesus. The apostle John said, "Love is made complete among us so that we will have confidence on the day of Judgment, because in this world we are like him" (1 John 4:17). Love is "made complete" in us as we are "made complete" in Christ.

Grow Up!

Read Psalm 92:12-14 in the margin. In the frame on page 115, draw a picture of what the psalmist says a righteous person is like. Next, make a list in the space provided of what he said will happen with a righteous person.

Grow Like a Cedar: Mount Lebanon

Lebanon is a mountain range marking the northern boundary of Canaan (Deut. 1:7; 3:25; 11:24). It extends north, parallel to the eastern Mediterranean coast. The name derives from the Hebrew word for *white*, owing to the white snow-capped peaks of the range (Jer. 18:14). The Lebanon mountains were famous not only for their beautiful white peaks, but also for their cedar forests, which were called "the glory" of Lebanon (Isa. 35:2; 60:13). The distinctive image of the cedar adorns the modern flag of the region.

The cedar is a magnificent, deep-rooted coniferous tree that grows for as many as two thousand years. It can reach massive diameters and heights (120 feet). Its fragrant wood is red in color and is especially durable and resistant to insects and decay. The wood was highly esteemed for its beauty and durability and was thus an important trade item in antiquity. King David used cedar in his palace (2 Sam. 5:11). King Solomon imported panels of cedar for building his palace and the temple in Jerusalem (1 Kings 5:6-10; 9:11; 2 Chron. 2:3). The Egyptians imported cedar for the tall, straight masts of their ships and for the durable coffins of their dead. King Nebuchadnezzar used it extensively for construction in his Babylonian empire.

Throughout the Old Testament, the cedar tree symbolizes grandeur (Ezek. 31:3) and majesty (2 Kings 14:9). The psalmist utilizes this imagery to illustrate his point: Those who love God "will grow like a cedar" (Ps. 92:12).

"A part of kindness consists in loving people more than they deserve." —Joseph Joubert[8] "Every one that has the power of godliness in his heart has his inclinations and heart exercised towards God and divine things, with such strength and vigor that these holy exercises do prevail in him above all carnal or natural affection." —Jonathan Edwards[9]

He or she will ...
• **flourish like a palm.**
•
•
•
•
•
•
•

Date palm trees grow to 40, 50, even 80 feet tall. The fibers of the tree are extremely elastic. Thus,

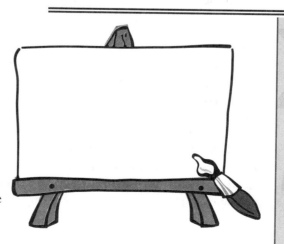

the tree trunk bends but does not break with the force of the wind. Feathery, green fronds—up to 20 feet long—crown the trunk. The fronds are a symbol of victory (Rev. 7:9). At Jesus' triumphal entrance into Jerusalem the crowds waved palm fronds (John 12:13).

The date palm is both beautiful and useful. It begins to bear fruit about 6 years after being planted, producing over 300 pounds of dates annually. It continues to be productive for over a century; and as the tree grows older, the fruit gets sweeter. In antiquity, the fibers from the base of the leaves were woven into ropes and rigging. The leaves were used to make brushes, mats, bags, couches, and baskets. Sap was processed into wine.

In the Holy Land, date palms were so abundant the Greeks and Romans called it "the land of the palms." The psalmist said a righteous person would "flourish" like a palm. The image is one of lasting strength, victory, beauty, and fruitfulness. The psalmist also said a righteous person would "grow" like a cedar of Lebanon. Did you draw a picture of a palm tree and a cedar above? To find out more, read today's High Point on Mount Lebanon on page 115.

What symptoms would alert you to the fact that a tree is dying? List them on the left below. What symptoms might indicate your love for God is dying? Write these on the right.

Symptoms of a Dying Tree	Symptoms of a Dying Love

I have three cedar trees in my backyard. Two are healthy and growing. The third is dead. Very dead. Beyond all hope dead. I know why it died. My black lab dog, Beau, decided this particular cedar made an excellent peeing post. Every time he needed to relieve himself, he'd run to that cedar and lift his leg.

It was a slow, agonizing death. That tree declined over two years. First, the lower boughs didn't look as green as they once did. Then, one whole section started turning yellow. Had I intervened at that point, the tree might have lived. But I procrastinated. Before I knew it, the whole cedar turned yellow and then brown. It's so dead and brittle now that it shatters when touched.

It's important to be attentive to the condition of your relationship with Christ. Is it fresh? Is it growing? Or is it dying? Once a year, I had my children stand against the same wall so I could measure how much they had grown. I couldn't tell the difference from day to day, but every year the mark up the wall got higher. Take a moment to fill out the growth chart in today's Climbing Gear, to see if you've grown in your love for the Lord.

Growth Chart

It's time for a spiritual check-up. Compare your current condition to a year ago. If you haven't changed, put an "X" on the midpoint of the line. If you've changed toward the characteristic on the left, mark an arrow pointing left (<) if you've changed toward the right, mark an arrow pointing right (>).

In the Past Year

My heart has hardened.	-------------- | --------------	My heart has softened.
I am more self-sufficient.	-------------- | --------------	I depend more on God.
I feel apathetic toward God.	-------------- | --------------	I long for God more.
The Bible bores me.	-------------- | --------------	I am excited about the Bible.
I feel detached during worship.	-------------- | --------------	My heart engages in worship.
I haven't felt convicted of sin.	-------------- | --------------	I have felt convicted of sin.
I can't think of sins I dealt with.	-------------- | --------------	I dealt with specific sins.
I hold grudges.	-------------- | --------------	I forgive others.
I am less tolerant.	-------------- | --------------	I have more compassion.
I feel less peace and joy.	-------------- | --------------	I feel more peace and joy.
I've become more critical.	-------------- | --------------	I've become more merciful.
I've become more indulgent.	-------------- | --------------	My self-control has increased.
I don't bear any spiritual fruit.	-------------- | --------------	I'm spiritually fruitful.
I talk to God less.	-------------- | --------------	I talk to God more.

Has your love for God grown the last year? ❑ yes ❑ no ❑ I'm not sure.

Unlike my cedar, we are never beyond all hope. God is gracious and merciful! Even if our love has decreased from burning fire to flickering ember, hope is not lost. With God's help, we can fan it back into flame (Rev. 2:4-5).

Pay attention to the condition of your heart. Press ever deeper into the burning love of Christ. That's the way to conquer the Mount of Affection. Close this week by asking God to help you love Him more. Take time to listen to what the Holy Spirit says to you. Jot your thoughts in the margin.

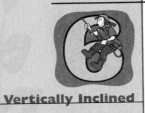

The Mount of Abundance:
Godward Climbers Delight in His Extravagance

a•bun•dance—Plentiful; ample; rich in supply; abounding; a fullness; great to overflowing; in profuse or extravagant degree.

Base Camp
Majestic mountains. A field strewn with boulders. A meadow adorned with wildflowers. Snowflakes. Stars. One need merely look around to see that when it comes to God, stingy and cheap are not descriptors that apply. God is unbelievably extravagant! This week we'll see that His extravagance enables us to live extravagantly! We can claim His hope and riches and power as our own.

Daily Lessons
Day 1: Mountains of Riches
  … Bequeathing an Extravagant Inheritance
 Day 2: Mountains of Favor
  … Giving an Extravagant Gift
Day 3: Mountains of Blessing
  … Receiving an Extravagant Measure
Day 4: Mountains of Resources
  … Accessing an Extravagant Supply
Day 5: Mountains of Joy
  … Climbing Toward an Extravagant Goal

High Points
- Rock of Israel
- Mount Ararat
- Mount Nebo
- Mount Bashan
- Mount Zion

Climbing Gear
- Grace-Hold
- Songs of Ascent

Memory Pack
"They feast on the abundance of your house; you give them drink from your river of delights. For with you is the fountain of life; in your light we see light" (Ps. 36:8-9).

The Mount of Abundance: Sheer Extravagance!

Ephesians 1:17-23

This Base Camp Guide will help you follow the video session for Summit 6.

1. He's an extravagant King.

   a. His realm is _____ _____ _____.
      (v. 21—"rule, authority, power, dominion")

   b. He's unbelievably _____. (v. 23—"fills everything")
     • blesses (v. 3), freely gives (v. 6), lavishes (v. 8)

2. He bestows an extravagant inheritance.

   a. Extravagant _____ (v. 18)

     • The _____ of _____ (Rom. 8:23-25; Col. 1:27)

   b. Extravagant _____ (v. 18)

     • _____ spiritual blessing (v. 3)

   c. Extravagant _____ (v. 19)

     • _____ _____ power

3. You can live like a prince or a pauper.

   a. Remain _____ of it. (v. 17—"wisdom/revelation")

   b. _____ it. (v. 17—"know him better")

   c. _____ it. (v. 18—"eyes closed")

   d. _____ it. (v. 23—"be filled")

Delight in His sheer extravagance. Claim His hope and riches and power as your own. That's the way to conquer the Mount of Abundance.

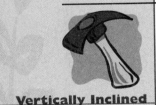

Mountains of Riches ...
Bequeathing an Extravagant Inheritance

Jack sat on the simple wooden bench in the mission and ate his soup without looking up. His clothes were dirty and much too large. His thin, gaunt face was stubbled with a couple of days growth. The large shopping bag at his feet contained all his worldly possessions: a tattered blanket, an old newspaper, a plastic cup, matches, a disposable razor, a wool hat, and a couple of soda cans he had picked up beside the road. There was nothing particular that would distinguish him from all the other homeless on Chicago's skid row.

It turned out to be Jack's last meal on earth. He died that night, poverty-stricken and friendless. He didn't know he had an inheritance of over four million dollars waiting for him in England. Though they had searched, the authorities were unable to locate him, for he had no address. An abundance of material wealth was his, yet Jack lived and died an impoverished beggar.

It's a tragic story, yet one that mirrors the sad reality of the lives of many believers. We live as spiritual paupers, unaware of the abundant riches that are ours in Christ. This week we're going to discover more about those riches, because every Godward climber ought to delight in His extravagance.

Heir to the King

By the end of this week's study, I hope you'll be challenged to tap into your spiritual inheritance and live like a prince instead of a pauper. But to truly understand the inheritance you've received in Christ, you first need to understand the inheritance that Christ, the Son of God, has received from His Father, "the great King" (Ps. 47:2).

Read Isaiah 40:21-26 and 1 Chronicles 29:11-12. Summarize ...

the extent of God's kingly rule: _____

the extent of God's kingly riches: _____

the extent of God's kingly power: _____

the extent of God's kingly majesty: _____

Hezekiah summed it up well when he exclaimed, "O Lord, God of Israel, enthroned between the cherubim, you alone are God over all the kingdoms of the earth" (2 Kings 19:15). Paul lauded the Father as the "blessed and only Sovereign, the King of kings and Lord of lords" whose dominion is eternal.

Read 1 Timothy 6:15-16 at right. Circle the phrase, "only Sovereign."

The word *sovereign* comes from the Latin "super," which means above/over, and "regnum," which refers to a kingdom. A sovereign is one who is supreme in power, possessing supreme dominion or jurisdiction, free of outside influence or control. God the Father is the "only" Sovereign. He is King over all. There is no limit placed on His authority. He has the right to establish all physical and moral laws by which all creatures are to be governed. He has the right to delegate authority. He has the right to appoint to each individual his position and lot. He determines when, where, and under what circumstances each individual is to be born, live, and die. He assigns them their heritage on earth and controls their destiny. Scripture tells us that He divides all mankind, sets up boundaries for the peoples, and gives the nations their inheritance (Deut. 32:8).

· ·

God's heir is His only begotten Son, Jesus. Read the verses below. In the column to the left, make a list of what the King has given His Son.

· ·

"In these last days [God] has spoken to us by his Son, whom he appointed heir of all things" (Heb. 1:2).

"[God] raised him from the dead and seated him at his right hand in the heavenly realms, far above all rule and authority, power and dominion, and every title that can be given, not only in the present age but also in the one to come. And God placed all things under his feet and appointed him to be head over everything" (Eph. 1:20-22).

"Jesus knew that the Father had put all things under his power, and that he had come from God and was returning to God" (John 13:3).

"He was given authority, glory and sovereign power ... His dominion is an everlasting dominion that will not pass away, and his kingdom is one that will never be destroyed" (Dan. 7:14).

"God was pleased to have all his fullness dwell in him" (Col 1:19).

"God exalted him to the highest place and gave him the name that is above every name" (Phil. 2:9).

Summit 6—
The Mount
of Abundance

"He who is the blessed and only Sovereign, the King of kings and Lord of lords, who alone possesses immortality and dwells in unapproachable light, whom no man has seen or can see. To Him be honor and eternal dominion! Amen" (1 Tim. 6:15-16, ESV).

121

Jesus claimed He had all authority: to forgive sins (Mark 2:10), to grant eternal life (John 17:2), to judge (John 5:27), to lay His life down and take it up again (John 10:17-18). He said, "All authority … has been given to me." "All things have been committed to me by my Father" (Matt. 28:18; 11:27).

As heir, Jesus received all authority, rule, power, dominion, and glory. God gave Him the name above all names and placed everything under His feet. All the fullness of the Father dwells in Him. That's why Jesus maintained that in seeing Him, the disciples had, in essence, seen the Father (John 14:8-10). The heir was a "chip off the Old Rock." Read more in today's High Point.

Chip off the Old Rock: Rock of Israel

In antiquity, the word *rock* brought to mind the security and defense of a steep, inaccessible fortress (Is. 32:2; 33:16). It also referred to a firm, immovable foundation (Ps. 40:2). It's no wonder then, that *rock* was used as a metaphor for God. Father God was called "the Rock of Israel" (2 Sam. 23:2). The Chaldaic form of the Hebrew word is sometimes translated "mountain."

The prophet Daniel had a vision of a rock cut out of a mountain. The rock grew to be a mountain that filled the earth (Dan. 2:35). The rock cut out of the mountain symbolized the coming of the Son of God. The Father gave His Son all rule, authority, power, and dominion. The vision looks forward to the time when everything will be made subject to Him and His kingdom will fill the whole earth.

In the New Testament, Jesus is identified as the "rock" the builders rejected and people stumble over, but that nevertheless has become the "chief cornerstone" (Matt. 21:42; Mark 12:10; Luke 20:17; Acts 4:11; 1 Pet. 2:7, ESV). The cornerstone is the large stone at the principal corner of a building. The whole building rests on it. In Jesus, the building blocks of prophets, apostles, and God's people all join together and rise to become the glorious house of God—the dwelling place of the King (Eph. 2:19-22).

"He is Sovereign of a far greater realm."—C.S. Lewis[1]

Master of the House

In the Old Testament, God often used people and objects as prophetic examples of the coming life and ministry of Jesus. Theologically, these are called "types" of Christ. Joshua and David were types of Christ, as were the Passover lamb and the serpent of brass that was lifted up on a pole. The type is an example that points towards the anti-type—Jesus.

In Isaiah 22:20-24 a man named Eliakim is a "type of Christ." Read the passage and fill in the following chart.

Symbol	Description	How this applies to Jesus
Robe	A royal robe or robe of office that distinguishes the wearer as having a position of honor and authority.	
Sash	The girdle in which the purse was carried. It was attached to the sword, and often adorned with gold and jewels.	
Key	The head of the house carried the keys hanging from a kerchief on the shoulder. He controlled access to the rooms of the house, including the treasury.	
Peg	Large pegs or poles stood in the center of ancient houses, providing the main support for the house. Containers and vessels were often hung on this peg.	
Seat	The seat of honor is a position or place of particular importance, giving special status to the person occupying it. The seat located at the head or center of the table as well as the seat to the right of that position were seats of honor.	

The Father has appointed His Son Heir and Master over His whole house. Jesus has unfathomable power, authority, rule, dominion, and riches. And He is filled with boundless love, joy, peace, truth, knowledge, wisdom, and grace—all the fullness of God! Close today's study by extolling Christ for everything He is, everything He has, and everything He has done.

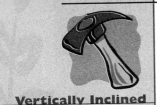

DAY 2

Mountains of Favor ...
Giving an Extravagant Gift

One day my young son, Matthew, came bolting through the front door yelling "Mom!!!" He was breathless and virtually coming undone at the seams with excitement. Jumping from foot to foot he finally managed, "Mom, you'll never guess what happened!" I was certain it must have been something very good, based on his enthusiasm. So I was shocked to hear that he had had an accident with his bike. He had taken his eyes off the road to try to fix a gear that was sticking, had swerved out of control, run into a parked car, and smashed its rear signal light.

"What? Where?" I exclaimed, confused. He obviously wasn't hurt. Was he simply happy that he hadn't gotten caught? The thoughts rapidly tumbled in my mind. "Show me where the car is. We have to find the owner. You'll have to apologize," I said sternly, "And you'll have to pay for the damage."

"No, you don't understand," Matt interrupted, laughing. "I already went. I knocked on the door right away to tell the man what I had done. He told me he was proud of me for coming to talk to him, and that I didn't have to pay for the repair; he would pay for it. Then he gave me a piece of gum."

My seven year-old had just experienced a gift of grace, and he was absolutely elated!

Unmerited Favor
Grace is the English translation of a Greek word (*charis*) meaning, "a favor which brings delight, joy, happiness, or good fortune." In classical Greek, the word referred to a freely conferred favor, with no expectation of return, motivated only by the generosity and big-heartedness of the giver.[2]

Briefly describe an instance when someone gave you a gift of grace.

_____

_____

New Testament writers use the word *grace* to describe the favor of God toward man. God the Father is called the "God of all grace" (1 Pet. 5:10), the Holy Spirit is called the "Spirit of grace" (Heb. 10:29), and Jesus Christ is described as being "full of grace" (John 1:14). All three give grace-gifts to us.

Read Ephesians 1:3-14,17-19. Fill in the blanks with the appropriate references.

The Father's grace-gifts:

- verse(s) _____ He chooses us.

- verse(s) _____ He adopts us.

- verse(s) _____ He richly blesses us.

The Son's grace-gifts:

- verse(s) _____ He redeems us.

- verse(s) _____ He forgives us.

- verse(s) _____ He reveals God's will to us.

The Spirit's grace-gifts:

- verse(s) _____ He seals us.

- verse(s) _____ He verifies our inheritance.

- verse(s) _____ He enables and empowers us.

Read more about God's grace in today's High Point.

"What he promises is more to be desired than all the world."
—John Piper[3]

Grace Boat: Mount Ararat

What would you do if you lived in a place as rainless as the Nevada Desert and the Lord instructed you to build a boat the size of two football fields to escape the coming flood? Would you believe Him, as Noah did? It took Noah many years to build that boat, but his faith saved him from the flood (Gen. 6–9).

After the flood subsided, the ark came to rest on Ararat. The mountains of Ararat are located between the Black and Caspian Seas in southern Armenia.

The name applied to the entire range, so it's not clear on which specific mountain the ark landed. However, a high, majestic mountain with two peaks, rising dramatically from the Araxes plain has been identified as the most likely location. The ancient Persians named it *Kuhinuh*, "Noah's mountain."

The Bible tells us Noah was saved by faith (Heb. 11:7). It also teaches that the ark passing through the floodwaters symbolized baptism, and how, through faith, people would be saved by the grace of God (1 Pet. 3:20-21). The waters of baptism illustrate Christ's death, burial, and resurrection. Noah was saved through faith by going through the floodwaters in the ark. But it is by God's grace that we are saved—through faith in the death, burial, and resurrection of Jesus.

God's grace is amazing! Even though I'm a self-centered sinner, He pours His favor upon me. He chooses me. I can't even begin to comprehend how or why. He forgives me, redeems me, adopts me into His family, and generously showers me with blessing upon blessing. God seals me with His Holy Spirit—His official stamp of approval and ownership, and the down payment on my inheritance. He enables and empowers me and gives me everything I need for life and godliness. I cannot begin to fathom the magnitude of His grace. And even more unfathomable is the fact that He lavishes such an overabundant amount on one so undeserving.

"Amazing grace! How sweet the sound."—John Newton[4]

Read Ephesians 2:8-9 in the margin. Mark the following statements true (T) or false (F.)

_____ **God's grace is a free gift. I'm not obligated to give Him anything in return.**
_____ **I'm saved through faith. Nothing I do can secure or lose my salvation.**
_____ **If I sin, I fall from grace. I must "clean up my act" to restore God's favor.**
_____ **If I displease Him enough, God will turn His back on me.**

God's got a "grace-hold" on us. Because of the sacrifice of Christ, He's able to offer us His gifts free of charge. We do not need to earn them or pay for them. Because of grace, simple faith in Jesus Christ saves us. There's nothing we can do to secure our salvation, and there's nothing we will do to lose it. My salvation is anchored on God's grace. Did you mark true for the first two statements and false for the last two? Find out more about the grace-hold of God in today's Climbing Gear on page 127.

Manifold Grace

Is there a relationship or situation in your life for which you feel you need God's grace? How do you think His promise of ALL grace in ALL things at ALL times could help you in that relationship or situation? Write your thoughts in the margin.

Summit 6—

The Mount of Abundance

- One blessing after another (John 1:16)
- Good and perfect gifts (Jas. 1:17)
- Power (2 Cor. 12:9)
- Hope and encouragement (2 Thess. 2:16)
- Wisdom and knowledge (Col. 3:2)
- Abundant life (John 10:10)
- Great joy (1 Pet. 1:8)
- Spiritual gifts (1 Pet. 4:10)

In 1 Peter 4:10, the apostle uses the Greek, *poikilos*, to describe God's grace. Several Bible versions translate the word with the adjective "mani-fold" (many-fold): "God's manifold grace." This indicates that God's grace manifests in many ways. Today we've taken a look at the major manifestations of God's grace, but there are lots of other grace-gifts that are part of the package. I listed a few beside the gift box above.

We'll talk more about the other grace-gifts throughout the week. But for now, close this lesson by thanking and praising God for His amazing grace.

Grace-Hold

Other than scaling a climbing wall in a gym, the video shoot of *Vertically Inclined* was the first time I had climbed. Someone asked me last week if I wasn't a little scared hanging off the side of a cliff. My answer was, "No, not the least bit." I had an absolute blast! I wasn't scared at all! The reason for my confidence was not my own skill—which, never having climbed, I obviously don't have. The reason for my confidence was my guide. We hired a certified, experienced mountain climber to help with the ropes, the knots, and the rigging. I knew he knew what he was doing. I had full confidence that his rope and knots were strong. I knew that even if I fell, the safety rope he had rigged would catch me. He was the reason for my confidence.

It's a great spiritual analogy! God is certified and experienced beyond measure, and He's got a grace-hold on you. He is "able to make all grace abound to you, … in all things, at all times." His grace gives you "ALL (my emphasis) you need" (2 Cor. 9:8). That's an amazing promise! The next time you feel like you're hanging on the side of a cliff, about to fall, remember the grace-hold of God. "To him who is able to keep you from falling and to present you before his glorious presence without fault and with great joy—to the only God our Savior be glory, majesty, power and authority, through Jesus Christ our Lord, before all ages, now and forevermore! Amen" (Jude 24-25). You've got His grace—so enjoy the climb!

127

Mountains of Blessing ...
Receiving an Extravagant Measure

"From the fullness of his grace we have all received one blessing after another" (John 1:16).

Living in the prairies, I'm quite accustomed to seeing cattle. But a couple of years ago I was taken aback to see huge, gangly ostriches strolling about a rural farmer's field. I was fascinated when, a short time later, a local farmer told me more about these birds.

The ostrich is the largest bird in the world. It can grow to 10 feet in height and weigh up to 400 pounds. One ostrich egg is equivalent to about 2-dozen chicken eggs. Hard-boiling one would take an hour and a half! Apparently, these birds can deliver a kick harder than soccer champ David Beckham. And they could outrun Olympian Carl Lewis. But according to the farmer, they're incredibly stupid. They exemplify the term, "bird-brain." In the harsh northern winter they'll stand helplessly, just outside the open door of the heated barn, and literally freeze to death. The barn offers warmth, shelter, and an abundance of food, but they're just too daft to go in.

My behavior is sometimes ostrich-like. God has given me an extravagant inheritance, yet often I fail to see or claim it. I helplessly poke my head in the sand and wallow in self-pity and defeat. This week we'll discover the riches we have in Christ. God is incredibly extravagant. His barn is full to the brim and overflowing. The door stands open. We need only step through and enter in.

Sheer Extravagance

Use the verse in the margin to answer the following questions.

WHO has received? _____

WHAT is received? _____

WHERE does this come from? _____

A few weeks ago, Brent and I moved our son, Matthew, out to the west coast to pursue his dream of a professional hockey career. Matt grew up on the prairies but now lives on a delta that juts out into the Pacific Ocean. I can't even begin to comprehend the enormity of the ocean. Walking in the salty waters along the shore, feeling wave after wave wash over my feet, I was overwhelmed by its vastness and constancy. Even more amazing was the thought that the mighty ocean is a scant drop in comparison to the fullness of the grace of God. It is from His fullness that we receive wave after wave of blessing—"one blessing after another." His blessings wash over those who believe with greater certainty than the waves of the ocean wash over the shore. As David exclaimed, "Surely you have granted [me] eternal blessings and made [me] glad with the joy of your presence" (Ps. 21:6).

Read Romans 10:12 in the margin. Have you called on the name of the Lord? Are you a follower of Jesus? If so, write your name in the following blanks to complete the sentences.

God richly blesses _____. **From the oceans of His grace**

_____ **has received wave upon wave of eternal blessings.**

Did you notice the adverb *richly*? God *richly* blesses. Our Father is neither stingy nor cheap. He is unbelievably extravagant toward His children. Jesus exemplified this family trait: at the wedding in Cana, He provided an overabundance of wine, at the picnic on the hill an overabundance of bread, in the disciples' net an overabundance of fish. The psalmist marveled at the sheer quantity of God's blessings, "Were I to speak and tell of them," he said, "they would be too many to declare" (Ps. 40:5).

The Bible uses several metaphors to describe the super-abundant blessings of God. In each frame, draw a picture to represent God's blessings.

like rain showers and flowing down like rivers (Ezek. 34:26; Ps. 78:15-16)

like carts overflowing with abundance (Ps. 65:11)

like vats overflowing with new wine and oil (Joel 2:24)

God's blessings are super abundant! over abundant! awesome! and even scary abundant! Jeremiah foretold that unbelievers would "be in awe" and "tremble" at the abundance God would pour out on His people (Jer. 33:9).

"There is no difference between Jew and Gentile—the same Lord is Lord of all and richly blesses all who call on him" (Rom. 10:12).

129

Blessings!

God's blessings are abundant. But what exactly is a blessing? In popular usage, the term can mean several things. It can express a wish for good fortune or happiness, like the pronouncement, "Bless you!" that follows a sneeze or the receipt of a gift. It can be an exclamation of surprise, "Oh, bless me!" My southern friends tell me that the word can also be used as a thinly veiled criticism, "Well, bless her heart." Blessing can refer to the prayer said before meals or the benediction pronounced after a meeting. Anyone who feels fortunate can use it as an expression of contentment, "I'm so blessed!"

The modern use of the term *bless* has somewhat obscured its original meaning. *Bless* comes from the old English *bledsian*. The first syllable *bled* means "blood." Hence, "blessing" was given when one person figuratively "gave blood" for another. The favor involved cost and self-sacrifice on the part of the giver. Scripture reveals that the blessings of God are specific, recognizable manifestations of divine favor centered in the death and resurrection of Christ (see Eph. 1:3-8). They are the grace-gifts we receive because of His shed blood.

In the margin, brainstorm a list of the blessings you've received in Christ.

We've received numerous blessings in Christ such as eternal life, love, joy, and peace. We'll talk more about them later, but for now I want you to understand that the blessings of God are firmly connected to the cross. His blessings are "blood-favors." The Bible teaches that those who lived before the death and resurrection of Christ received God's blessing in anticipation of that promised event. "These were all commended for their faith, yet none of them received what had been promised" (Heb. 11:39). Moses is cited as an example. Find out more about Moses and his anticipation of God's blessing in today's High Point on page 131, featuring Mount Nebo, the mountain on which Moses died.

Moses was only able to look forward to the fulfillment of the promise. For us, the promise has already been fulfilled (Heb. 11:39-40). The Greek word translated "have received" indicates an ongoing process that encompasses past, present, and future. Through Jesus, all of God's blessings are already ours. We have received them in their entirety. At the same time, we will not completely receive them until the second coming of Christ.

Theologians use a special phrase to describe this tension: "the now and not yet." The best way I can think to explain it is this: We live in the period of time between the receipt of a gift and the complete unpacking of that gift. Through Jesus, I've received the gift of God. The whole package is fully and completely mine. Some of the wrapping is already off—enough so I can tell what the gift contains. I enjoy it now, but I won't get to fully enjoy it until it's completely unwrapped. And that won't happen until Jesus returns.

Blessings Promised: Mount Nebo

As instructed, Moses climbed the mountain that bordered the plain of Moab, east of the Jordan River. He knew it would be a one-way trip. He had brought the people as far as he could. They were camped on the border ready to enter. The blessings had been pronounced, the promises reconfirmed. Though he was 120 years old, the man's eyes had not dimmed, nor had his strength diminished. Using the smooth, weathered staff for balance, he clambered up the rock from foothold to foothold. He had an appointment to keep.

The day was clear, the view from the summit majestic. He turned to the east, toward the sparkling waters of the Dead Sea, and drank in the sight. At long last he could see in the distance what he had only dreamed of: the promised land. His eyes misted with tears as his Friend pointed out the landmarks. Gilead as far as Dan, all Napthali, the land of Ephraim and Manasseh, all the land of Judah as far as the Western Sea, the Negeb, and Jericho, in the valley of palms. It was unbelievable! So lush and green! A land of milk and honey, to be certain. The blessings of God right before his eyes! A gentle sigh escaped his lips. The people would enter without him. He knew that full well. But it was all right. Moses knew that though he could only enjoy it from afar, the promise had, in essence, already been granted. So sure and certain was God's word. The land was indeed beautiful, but the beauty of another land beckoned. It was time to enter in. Moses smiled. Contented, he turned and extended his arms (Deut. 34:1-4; Num. 20:2-12).

Summit 6—

The Mount of Abundance

"Praise be to the God and Father of our Lord Jesus Christ, who has blessed us in the heavenly realms with every spiritual blessing in Christ" (Eph. 1:3)

"In God there is no hunger that needs to be filled, only plenteousness that desires to give."
—C.S. Lewis[5]

The "now and not yet" is an important concept. To enjoy God's extravagance, you need to realize you possess all of His blessings in full measure. Abundant love is yours. Abundant joy is yours. Abundant peace is yours. Wistfully wishing for these things, or searching for them elsewhere, is like the ostrich freezing to death outside while the warmth of the barn beckons.

In closing, read Ephesians 1:3. Thank God for blessing you abundantly with every spiritual blessing in Christ.

DAY 4

Mountains of Resources ...
Accessing an Extravagant Supply

Vertically Inclined

"He who did not spare his own Son, but gave him up for us all—how will he not also, along with him, graciously give us all things?" (Rom. 8:32).

What would you do if you suddenly inherited several million dollars? Jot some ideas in the margin.

Hetty Green received a big inheritance from her father. By the time of her death in 1896, she was said to be the richest woman in the world. But strangely, Hetty refused to touch her inheritance. She didn't want to spend a penny on herself, on her family, or on others. Instead, she lived as a miserly pauper.

What would you do if you inherited a large sum of money? Imagine the possibilities! You could pay off debts, buy a new car, pay for your child's education, give gifts, invest the principle and retire on the interest, donate the money to a worthy cause, or help the needy. There are lots of possibilities. But you would be very foolish indeed if you had all that money and did absolutely nothing with it. Yet unfortunately, "nothing" is precisely what we often do with our spiritual inheritance. God has given us vast spiritual wealth, yet so many of us are like the servant in the parable: we bury it in the ground and ignore it (Matt. 25:14-30). We live as paupers when we should be living as princes.

Read Romans 8:15-17. How does Paul describe a believer's relationship to God? Check all that apply.

❑ child of God   ❑ heir of God
❑ co-heir with Christ   ❑ distant relative

Every believer is a child of God and thus, an heir of God and co-heir with Christ.

Read Romans 8:32 in the margin. Circle the words that describe the inheritance God the Father has given you.

God the Father isn't stingy. He's given you an inheritance of unfathomable proportions. Did you circle the words, "his own Son," and "all things"? You've received Christ, and along with Him, all of His riches. The whole package is yours. You are rich! A spiritual billionaire! Read more about being rich in today's High Point.

Rich Mountain, Poor Mountain: Mount Bashan

Rich. Rich. Rich. That's the way to describe Bashan. Bashan was the name of a region northeast of Palestine that stretched from the plateau of south Syria across the Yarmuk River to the foothills of Gilead. It encompassed the lower part of the Anti-Lebanon mountain range, which includes the towering peak of Hermon. In pre-Israelite times, Bashan was the territory of the famed, Og, King of Bashan, a giant of a man, whose iron bed was more than 13 feet long and 6 feet wide (Deut. 3:10-14).

The plain of Bashan was incredibly fertile, blanketed with rich vineyards, orchards, fields of grain, and pastures (Jer. 50:19). The fatness of the region's livestock was proverbial (Deut. 32:14; Ps. 22:12; Ezek. 39:18; Amos 4:1). The luxurious bounty of Bashan extended into the mountains, where the slopes were thickly carpeted with majestic oak forests (Isa. 2:13). These oaks were highly prized throughout the ancient world for construction and were used to make the long, sturdy oars of the great Phoenician trade ships (Ezek. 27:6).

Bashan's riches were unmatched. Yet the psalmist argues that Mount Bashan gazes in envy at Mount Zion, the dwelling place of God (Ps. 68:15-16). Physically, the mountains of Bashan were 2 to 3 times the height of Jerusalem's Mount Zion, and the region was arguably 10 times richer in resources. But compared to the enormous riches of God, and the abundant blessings He bestows, Bashan is small, insignificant, and poor. Through Christ, God gives believers gifts that far exceed the greatest wealth on earth. (Eph. 4:7).

"Faith is a living, daring confidence in God's grace, so sure and certain that a man could stake his life on it a thousand times."
—Martin Luther[6]

Like a Prince or Pauper?

The riches that are yours in Christ exceed the greatest wealth on earth. Are you tapping into your spiritual inheritance?

The following list itemizes some of the riches you have. For each treasure, put a mark on the continuum, indicating the extent to which you are accessing and enjoying that resource.

1. Abundant life (John 10:10)

I'm living like a pauper.   **I'm living like a prince.**

2. Abundant love (Jude 2; 1 Thess. 3:12)

I'm living like a pauper.   **I'm living like a prince.**

133

3. Abundant peace (1 Pet. 1:2; Rom. 15:13)

I'm living like a pauper.   **I'm living like a prince.**

4. Abundant joy (1 Pet. 1:8; Phil 1:26)

I'm living like a pauper.   **I'm living like a prince.**

5. Abundant comfort (2 Cor. 1:3,5)

I'm living like a pauper.   **I'm living like a prince.**

6. Abundant strength (Eph. 1:19; 6:10)

I'm living like a pauper.   **I'm living like a prince.**

7. Abundant hope (Eph. 1:18; Col. 1:27)

I'm living like a pauper.   **I'm living like a prince.**

8. Abundant delight (Ps. 36:8)

I'm living like a pauper.   **I'm living like a prince.**

9. Abundant wisdom (Jas. 1:5)

I'm living like a pauper.   **I'm living like a prince.**

10. Abundant generosity (Phil. 4:19; 2 Cor. 8:2)

I'm living like a pauper.   **I'm living like a prince.**

11. Abundant self-discipline (2 Tim. 1:7)

I'm living like a pauper.   **I'm living like a prince.**

12. Abundant forgiveness (Eph. 1:7-8)

I'm living like a pauper.   **I'm living like a prince.**

13. Abundant righteousness (2 Cor. 6:7; 9:9-10)

I'm living like a pauper.   **I'm living like a prince.**

14. Abundant mercy (Eph. 1:6; 2:4)

I'm living like a pauper   **I 'm living like a prince**

15. Abundant power (Eph. 1:19)

I'm living like a pauper.   **I'm living like a prince.**

Circle the three riches you would like to experience more.

Open the Eyes of My Heart

Don't feel guilty if some or all of your marks gravitated toward the left side of the scale. God does not condemn us for this. But He does want you and me to learn to live richly, as children of the King of the universe. The question is not whether we are spiritually rich. According to Scripture, we are rich. Rather, the question is whether we believe we are, and whether we choose to live like we are.

I can choose hope; I can choose joy; and I can choose peace, because the blood of Jesus has paid the price to put all these things into my account. Everything that is His is mine. He said so, and I believe Him. I choose to trust and believe Him even when every circumstance challenges my resolve. I'm not saying it's easy. I know full well just how tough it can be.

This year has been incredibly difficult. Last Christmas Eve, my entire family was in a car accident. Almost all of us sustained neck and back injuries. Since that time, I've struggled with pain and excruciating headaches on a daily basis. I won't go into details, but the car accident wasn't the only challenge I faced. It's been a tough year. Real tough. I remember lying in bed one night, crying and lamenting to Brent about the sorry state of affairs. He listened as I droned on and on about all my troubles. After I had exhausted all my complaints, he wiped the tears from my face and quietly said, "But Mary, we're SO rich!"

It's true. God the Father has given us His Son, and along with Him, has graciously given us all things. We live in the time of the "now and not yet." We have not yet seen it all, but even now, we are able to enjoy our vast inheritance. I pray, along with Paul, "that the eyes of your heart may be enlightened in order that you may know the hope to which he has called you, the riches of his glorious inheritance in the saints and his incomparably great power for us who believe" (Eph. 1:18-19).

"Faith sees the invisible, believes the incredible and receives the impossible."—Anonymous[7]

Vertically Inclined

Mountains of Joy ...
Climbing Toward an Extravagant Goal

"Keep your eyes on the goal," is the oft-repeated advice by coaches of sport and of life. In this study, our goal has been to explore the seven summits of successful godward climbers. Today, you'll do the last daily lesson. In a way, we've reached our goal. But in another way, this end is only the beginning. The theme verse of this study teaches us that there's a much greater goal on which to fix our eyes:

One thing I do, forgetting those things which are behind and reaching forward to those things which are ahead, I press toward the goal for the prize of the upward call of God in Christ Jesus (Phil. 3:13-14, NKJV).

According to this passage, what's the greatest goal?

_____

_____

We can pursue the upward call of God by continually pushing higher up the seven summits that we explored in this study: the Mounts of Anticipation, Allegiance, Appraisal, Affliction, Affection, Abundance, and Adventure. But the goal of the upward call—and the whole motivation of our climb—is the extravagant PRIZE that awaits us at the summit.

Eyes on the Prize
The writer of Hebrews was concerned that his friends keep their eyes on the prize of the inheritance of God. He warned them against being distracted by lesser goals. He cited the example of Esau, who for the sake of immediate gratification traded his entire inheritance for a meager bowl of soup. Esau missed receiving the blessing because he didn't keep his eye on the prize (Heb. 12:16-17).

Read Hebrews 12:16-24. According to verse 22, where's the prize?

_____

_____

The City of the Great King: Mount Zion

The loyalties of the fledgling nation of Israel were divided after Saul, its first king, was killed in battle. Ish-Bosheth, Saul's surviving son, claimed the throne in the northern state of Israel (2 Sam. 2:10), while David was recognized as king over the southern state of Judah (2 Sam. 2:4). For 7 years the two waged a bloody civil war. In the end, Ish-Bosheth was defeated, and David was declared king of both Israel and Judah (2 Sam. 5:3).

David wanted to consolidate his kingdom and bring peace and unity to the warring factions. To do this, he and his army stormed and conquered a Canaanite stronghold geographically situated between Israel and Judah. The fortress city of Jebus (1 Chron. 11:4)—occupied by Jebusites—was located on the hill of Zion. Neither the northern nor southern armies had been able to completely subdue it. But in a brilliant scheme, David and his men entered the fortress through water tunnels by night, taking it by surprise (2 Sam. 5:8).

David claimed the city as his own—"the City of David" (2 Sam. 5:9). It became an independent city-state, belonging exclusively to the monarchy. This was a highly strategic move. To begin, David established a kingly residence for himself in a neutral location, thus avoiding the necessity of choosing between the north and south. Furthermore, he geographically united the kingdom by removing the Canaanite barrier between the two states. The City of David, located on the hill of Zion, was named Jerusalem.[8] It became the political and spiritual center for the entire Jewish nation.

The Hebrew word *Zion* may mean "citadel" or "fortress." At first, Zion referred only to the southeast ridge on which David's city of Jerusalem stood—including the place where David pitched a tent for the ark of the covenant (1 Chron. 15:1). Its meaning later expanded to include the entire city and even the mount on which Solomon's temple stood (Mount Moriah).

Zion also took on a metaphorical meaning. The bringing up of the ark and building of the temple established Zion as God's dwelling place. It was the city of the king—King David. But it also came to symbolize the spiritual and heavenly city of the Great King—the King of Kings—the eternal dwelling place of God (Ezek. 48:35).

The writer of Hebrews explained that the believers had "come to Mount Zion, to the heavenly Jerusalem, the city of the living God." Do you remember the theological phrase "the now and not yet"? The believers had come—in other words, they had already received their inheritance (now). But obviously, they had not yet seen it all, for they were still living in Rome and not in heaven.

137

On the mountain to the right, make a list of who the believers were told they would someday see on Mount Zion (vv. 22-24).

Read more about Mount Zion and Jerusalem in today's High Point on page 137.

In the heavenly Jerusalem, we will see thousands and thousands of angels in joyful assembly. Have you ever seen a joyful assembly? The most joyful assembly I ever saw was when my son's hockey team won the division title. They were pretty joyful! But can you imagine thousands upon thousands of angels in joyful assembly? The thought absolutely boggles my mind.

On that mount, we will also see the church—throngs and throngs of people whose names are written in heaven: Paul will be there, Mary and John, Moses, Ruth, David, Anna, and the woman the Pharisee deemed too unclean to eat at his table. Martin Luther, Jonathan Edwards, C. S. Lewis, and Corrie Ten Boom will be there. And so will my grandparents, my mom and dad, and all my relatives and friends who loved the Lord. I wonder who'll make more joyful noise! The angels?—or the people?

Jeremiah prophetically compared the scene to the time the Jews returned from exile: "They will come and shout for joy on the heights of Zion; they will rejoice in the bounty of the LORD—the grain, the new wine and the oil, the young of the flocks and herds. They will be like a well-watered garden, and they will sorrow no more. Then maidens will dance and be glad, young men and old as well. I will turn their mourning into gladness; I will give them comfort and joy instead of sorrow. I will satisfy the priests with abundance, and my people will be filled with my bounty," declares the LORD (Jer. 31:12-14).

Can you imagine the joy of the heavenly Zion? Can you imagine the riches? Can you imagine the party? The thought is absolutely overwhelming. But even more unfathomable than all the angels, people, and riches is this: We will see Jesus. And we will see our Almighty Father God … face-to-face.

Crossing the Finish to Glory

The 1992 Summer Olympics in Barcelona will always stand out in my mind because of one poignant event. It was near the end of the men's 400-meter race. Derrick Redmond, from Great Britain, suddenly collapsed on the track clutching his right hamstring. He writhed in pain as the other runners raced past. Officials moved toward Redmond to assist him off the track, but Derrick shouted them away. In excruciating pain, and with tears streaming down his face, he struggled to his feet and began to slowly and agonizingly

Songs of Ascent

Psalms 120–134 are called songs of ascent. They formed a book of songs sung by pilgrims going up to Jerusalem for the annual feasts of Passover, Pentecost, and Tabernacles. Lifting one's eyes up and journeying to Zion to meet God is the oft repeated theme. Next time you sing a song of worship, think of it as a song of ascent. Your life is a joyful journey up to the heavenly Mount Zion—your heart's true home—where you will dwell with God.

Read Revelation 21:1-7 and 22:1-5 to get more of a glimpse of the prize that awaits us. The fulfillment of every desire is found in Christ. He is the goal of our deepest quest. Our longings for love, joy, peace, acceptance, beauty, wisdom, strength, and abundance are all fulfilled in Him.

"In the end the heart longs not for any of God's good gifts, but for God himself."—John Piper[9]

inch down the lane. Though the other runners had long since crossed the line, it was obvious that Derrick was still bent on completing the race. The crowd watched in stunned silence. Suddenly, a stout middle-aged man jumped out of the stands, dashed past security officials, ran onto the track, and propped the injured runner up. The man was Derek's father. Fighting off security, the Redmonds moved toward the finish together—the son, leaning heavily and sobbing with pain; the father, crying tears of his own, yet lending strong support and gentle words of encouragement. Derrick crossed the line 4 minutes and 16 seconds after the gold medal winner. The crowd gave him an unrivaled ovation. The burly father then picked his son up in both arms and took him for medical care.

The spiritual parallels are evident. To begin, the son was determined to make it to the finish, regardless of the cost. He refused to quit before he reached the goal. That's the kind of determination it takes for godward climbers to keeping straining upward toward the prize. Another parallel is the deep love and commitment of the Father to help his son make it. Our heavenly Father has an even deeper commitment toward us. And when we cross that finish line with Him, He will scoop us up in His arms, heal every hurt—wipe away every tear, and with great joy, lead us into glory. Thousands upon tens of thousands of angels will erupt in joyful celebration. At long last we will be united with the One who loves us so extravagantly, and for whom our hearts have so desperately yearned. We will see Him face-to-face and be overwhelmed and overjoyed in the wonder of His presence.

The prize is worth all the effort! So keep reaching for those things which are ahead. Press toward the goal, and keep your heart vertically inclined.

The Mount of Adventure
Godward Climbers Press Upward and Forever Upward

ad•ven•ture—An exciting experience; a daring enterprise; a bold and extraordinary undertaking. v. to venture on, to attempt. Have you embarked on the Great Adventure?

There's nothing more thrilling than the adventure of climbing higher with God. Continually reaching forward and pressing toward "the goal for the prize of the upward call of God in Christ" is life's ultimate challenge and ultimate joy.

"The first question which you will ask and which I must try to answer is this, 'What is the use of climbing Everest?' ... if you cannot understand that there is something in man which responds to the challenge of this mountain and goes out to meet it, that the struggle is the struggle of life itself upward and forever upward, then you won't see why we go. What we get from this adventure is just sheer joy."
—George Leigh Mallory, 1922[1]

Summit 7—
The Mount of Adventure

This Base Camp Guide will help you follow the video session for Summit 7.

Secrets of an Extreme Adventurer
Philippians 3:12-14

1. Reach for what you've been _____ _____.

2. Press upward and _____ _____.

   a. Be _____-_____

   b. Be _____-_____

   c. Be _____-_____

3. Do it for the _____.

"Forgetting those things which are behind and reaching forward to those things which are ahead, I press toward the goal for the prize of the upward call of God in Christ Jesus" (Phil. 3:13-14, NKJV).

Vertically Inclined: Seven Summits

7

Adventure
Godward Climbers Press Upward and Forever Upward

6

Abundance
Godward Climbers Delight in His Extravagance

5

Affection
Godward Climbers Keep Their Love Alive

4

Affliction
Godward Climbers Persevere Through Difficulty

3

Appraisal
Godward Climbers Evaluate and Make Adjustments

2

Allegiance
Godward Climbers are Loyal to His Standard

1

Anticipation
Godward Climbers Anticipate an Encounter with Christ

In the last days the mountain of the LORD's temple will be established as chief among the mountains; it will be raised above the hills, and all nations will stream to it (Isa. 2:2).

On this mountain the LORD Almighty will prepare a feast of rich food for all peoples, a banquet of aged wine-the best of meats and the finest of wines. On this mountain he will destroy the shroud that enfolds all peoples, the sheet that covers all nations; he will swallow up death forever. The Sovereign LORD will wipe away the tears from all faces; he will remove the disgrace of his people from all the earth. The LORD has spoken. In that day they will say, "Surely this is our God; we trusted in him, and he saved us. This is the LORD, we trusted in him; let us rejoice and be glad in his salvation" (Isa. 25:6-9).

I lift up my eyes to the hills-where does my help come from? (Ps. 121:1).

Ararat
16,873 ft.

Lebanon
10,540 ft.

Hermon
(Bashan)
9232 ft.

Sinai
(Horeb)
6888 ft.

Ebal
3100 ft.

Nebo
2706 ft

Olives
2657 ft.

Zion
(Moriah)
2451 ft.

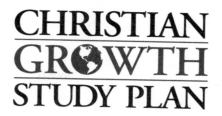

CHRISTIAN GROWTH STUDY PLAN

In the **Christian Growth Study Plan (formerly Church Study Course),** this book *Vertically Inclined: Climbing Higher with God* is a resource for course credit in the subject area Personal Life of the Christian Growth category of plans. To receive credit, read the book, complete the learning activities, show your work to your pastor, a staff member or church leader, then complete the following information. This page may be duplicated. Send the completed page to:

Christian Growth Study Plan
One LifeWay Plaza • Nashville, TN 37234-0117
FAX: (615)251-5067
E-MAIL: *cgspnet@lifeway.com*
For information about the Christian Growth Study Plan, refer to the Christian Growth Study Plan Catalog. It is located online at *www.lifeway.com/cgsp.* If you do not have access to the Internet, contact the Christian Growth Study Plan office (1.800.968.5519) for the specific plan you need for your ministry.

VERTICALLY INCLINED: CLIMBING HIGHER WITH GOD
COURSE NUMBER: CG-1029

PARTICIPANT INFORMATION

Social Security Number (USA ONLY-optional)

Personal CGSP Number*

Date of Birth (MONTH, DAY, YEAR)

Name (First, Middle, Last)

Home Phone

Address (Street, Route, or P.O. Box)

City, State, or Province

Zip/Postal Code

Please check appropriate box: ❑ Resource purchased by self ❑ Resource purchased by church ❑ Other

CHURCH INFORMATION

Church Name

Address (Street, Route, or P.O. Box)

City, State, or Province

Zip/Postal Code

CHANGE REQUEST ONLY

❑ Former Name

❑ Former Address

City, State, or Province

Zip/Postal Code

❑ Former Church

City, State, or Province

Zip/Postal Code

Signature of Pastor, Conference Leader, or Other Church Leader

Date

*New participants are requested but not required to give SS# and date of birth. Existing participants, please give CGSP# when using SS# for the first time. Thereafter, only one ID# is required. **Mail to:** Christian Growth Study Plan, One LifeWay Plaza, Nashville, TN 37234-0117. Fax: (615)251-5067.

Rev. 3-03

Endnotes

Summit 1
Day 1

1) *New Bible Dictionary*, 1996, 3rd Ed. Libronix.com ref. Mount, Mountain
2) Libronix Digital Library, Harris, Archer & Waltke, *Theological Wordbook of the Old Testament*, 1999, Moody Press, 1708a.
3) Jonathan Waterman, ed., *The Quotable Climber* (New York, NY: The Lions Press, 1998), 41.
4) Ibid., 21.

Day 2

5) John Bartlett, *Familiar Quotations*, 10th ed., #4248, [online], 10 October 2002. Available from Internet: *http://www.Bartleby.com*.
6) Piper, John, *Desiring God* (Portland, OR: Multnomah, 1986), 213.

Day 3

7) George Mallory, "Quotes from Everest," [online], 8 October 2003. Available from Internet: *http://www.mnteverest.net*.
8) Ibid.
9) Wayne Martindale and Jerry Root, eds., *The Quotable Lewis*, #1002 (Wheaton, IL: Tyndale House, 1989), 406.
10) J. Swanson, *Dictionary of Biblical Languages with Semantic Domains*, Definition #2675, Hebrew (Old Testament), (Oak Harbor: Logos Research Systems, Inc., 1997).
11) Ibid.
12) Steve Gardiner, *Why I Climb* (Harrisburg, PA: Stackpole Books, 1990), 51.

Day 4

13) The Midrash, ancient Jewish rabbinical writings, says the Shekinah lingered for 3 1/2 years (Lamentations Rabba, Proem 25)
14) Edmond Clarence Stedman, ed., *An American Anthology*, #328, [online], 28 October 2002. Available from Internet: *http://www.Bartleby.com*.

15) John Bartlett and Emily Morrison Beck eds., *Bartlett's Familiar Quotations*, #6 (Boston, MA: Little, Brown and Company, 1980), 729.

Day 5

16) CFL is the Canadian Football League. Brent is chaplain for the Edmonton Eskimos.
17) Thomas À Kempis, *The Imitation of Christ* (Harmondsworth, Middlesex, England: Penguin Books, 1952), 121.
18) Wayne Martindale and Jerry Root, eds., *The Quotable Lewis*, #978 (Wheaton, IL: Tyndale House, 1989), 400.

Summit 2
Day 1

1) The major biblical covenants are the Edenic (Genesis 2:16), Adamic (Genesis 3:15), Noahic (Genesis 9:16), Abrahamic (Genesis 12:2), Mosaic (Exodus 19:5), Palestinian (Deuteronomy 30:3), and New Covenant (Hebrews 8:8).
2) Frank S. Mead, ed., *12,000 Religious Quotations* (Grand Rapids, MI: Baker Book House, 1989), 187.

Day 2

3) Albert M. Wells Jr., ed., *Inspiring Quotations, Contemporary and Classical*, #634 (Nashville, TN: Thomas Nelson, 1988), 52-53.

Day 3

4) R.V.G. Tasker, *The Second Epistle of Paul to the Corinthians: An Introduction and Commentary*, (Grand Rapids, MI: InterVarsity, Wm. B. Eerdmans, 1983), 49.
5) Isaac Watts, "When I Survey the Wondrous Cross" *Baptist Hymnal* (Nashville, TN: Convention Press, 1991), 144.
6) George Sweeting, ed., *Great Quotes and Illustrations* (Waco, TX: World Books Publisher, 1985), 172.

Day 4

7) Frank S. Mead, ed., *12,000 Religious Quotations* (Grand Rapids, MI: Baker Book House, 1989), 320.
8) A. Robertson, *Word Pictures in the New Testament* (Oak Harbor: Logos Research Systems, 1997), Matt. 5:1.

Day 5

9) Frederick W. Faber, "Faith of Our Fathers," *The Baptist Hymnal* (Nashville, TN; Convention Press, 1991), 352.
10) Albert M. Wells Jr., ed., *Inspiring Quotations, Contemporary and Classical*, #858 (Nashville, TN: Thomas Nelson, 1988), 69.

Summit 3
Day 1

1) Jon Krakauer, "Quotes from Everest," [online], 8 October 2002. Available from Internet: *http://www.mnteverest.net/quote/html*.
2) Jonathan Waterman, ed., *The Quotable Climber* (New York, NY: The Lions Press, 1998), 144.

Day 2

3) Jonathan Waterman, ed., *The Quotable Climber* (New York, NY: The Lions Press, 1998), 95.
4) Albert M. Wells Jr., ed., *Inspiring Quotations, Contemporary and Classical*, #1174 (Nashville, TN: Thomas Nelson, 1988), 92.

Day 3

5) George Sweeting, ed., *Great Quotes and Illustrations* (Waco, TX: World Books Publisher, 1985), 210.
6) Cory Lloyd, ed., *Quotable Quotations* (Wheaton, IL: Victor Books, 1989), 303.

Day 4

7) Albert M. Wells Jr., ed., *Inspiring Quotations Contemporary and Classical*, #1170 (Nashville, TN: Thomas Nelson, 1988), 91.

8) George Sweeting, ed., *Great Quotes and Illustrations* (Waco, TX: World Books Publisher, 1985), 145-146.

Day 5

9) Albert M. Wells Jr., ed., *Inspiring Quotations, Contemporary and Classical*, #1167 (Nashville, TN: Thomas Nelson, 1988), 91.

10) Ibid., 91-92.

Summit 4
Day 1

1) George Sweeting, ed., *Great Quotes and Illustrations* (Waco, TX: World Books Publisher 1985), 243.

2) Bruce Cockburn, "Waiting for a Miracle: Singles 1970-1987" Track 14: "Laughter" (High Romance Music,1987).

3) Frank S. Mead, ed., *12,000 Religious Quotations* (Grand Rapids, MI: Baker Book House, 1989), 323.

Day 2

4) Sally Jenkins, "Extra Ordinary Ways Unseen," [online], 11 August 2003. Available from Internet: *http://www.washingtonpost.com*.

5) "Lance Armstrong – A Bibliography," [online], 11 August 2003. Available from Internet: *http://www.lancearmstrong.com*.

6) Sally Jenkins, "Extra Ordinary in Ways Unseen," [online], ll August 2003. Available from Internet: *http://www.washingtonpost.com/wp-dyn/articles/A54327*.

7) Ibid.

8) Ibid.

9) George Sweeting, ed., *Great Quotes and Illustrations* (Waco, TX: World Books Publisher, 1985), 243.

10) Ibid., 243.

Day 3

11) Eleanor Doan, ed., *Speakers Sourcebook II* (Grand Rapids, MI: Ministry Resources Library, 1968), 338.

12) Carroll E. Simcox, ed., *3000 Quotations on Christian Themes*, #1828 (Grand Rapids, MI: Baker Book House, 1975), 156.

Day 4

13) ©Corrie ten Boom Foundation, "History," [online], 3 September 2003. Available from Internet: *http://www.corrietenboom.com*.

14) Augustus M. Toplady, "Rock of Ages," *The Baptist Hymnal* (Nashville, TN; Convention Press, 1991), 352.

15) Eleanor Doan, ed., *Speakers Sourcebook* (Grand Rapids, MI: Ministry Resources Library, 1960), 64.

Day 5

16) Albert M. Wells Jr., ed., *Inspiring Quotations, Contemporary and Classical*, #2546 (Nashville, TN: Thomas Nelson, 1988), 192.

Summit 5
Day 1

1) Albert M. Wells, Jr., ed., *Inspiring Quotations, Contemporary and Classical*, #1547 (Nashville, TN: Thomas Nelson, 1988), 117.

2) Eleanor Doan, ed., *Speakers Sourcebook II* (Grand Rapids, MI: Ministry Resources Library, 1968), 248.

Day 2

3) Frank S. Mead, ed., *12,000 Religious Quotations* (Grand Rapids, MI: Baker Book House, 1989), 320.

4) M. Easton, *Easton's Bible Dictionary* (Oak Harbor, WA: Logos Research Systems Inc., 1996).

5) Frank S. Mead, ed., *12,000 Religious Quotations* (Grand Rapids, MI: Baker Book House, 1989), 320.

Day 3

6) Carroll E. Simcox, ed., *3000 Quotations on Christian Themes*, #2316 (Grand Rapids, MI: Baker Book House, 1975), 192.

Day 4

7) Eleanor Doan, ed., *Speakers Sourcebook II* (Grand Rapids, MI: Ministry Resources Library, 1968), 256.

8) George Sweeting, ed., *Great Quotes and Illustrations* (Waco, TX: World Books Publisher, 1985), 178.

Day 5

9) Jonathan Edwards, *The Religious Affections* (Carlisle, PA: The Banner of Truth Trust, 1986), 28-29.

Summit 6
Day 1

1) Wayne Martindale and Jerry Root, eds., *The Quotable Lewis*, #606 (Wheaton, IL: Tyndale, 1989), 262.

Day 2

2) K.S. Wuest, (1997, c1984). Wuest word studies from the *Greek New Testament: for the English Reader* (Grand Rapids, MI: Eerdmans, Libronix Digital Library System).

3) John Piper, *Desiring God* (Portland, OR: Multnomah, 1986), 55.

4) John Newton, "Amazing Grace! How Sweet the Sound," *The Baptist Hymnal* (Nashville, TN; Convention Press, 1991), 352.

Day 3

5) Wayne Martindale and Jerry Root, eds., *The Quotable Lewis*, #606 (Wheaton, IL: Tyndale, 1989), 262.

Day 4

6) George Sweeting, ed., *Great Quotes and Illustrations* (Waco, TX: World Books, 1985), 111.

7) Albert M. Wells Jr., ed., *Inspiring Quotations, Contemporary and Classical*, #856 (Nashville, TN: Thomas Nelson, 1988), 69.

Day 5

8) Kings often renamed the territories they conquered. The city of Jerusalem was formerly called Jebus for the Jebusites that controlled it (1 Chron. 11:4). Another name for the city was Haeleph (Josh. 18:28).

9) John Piper, *Desiring God* (Portland, OR: Multnomah, 1986), 56.

Summit 7

1) George Mallory, "Quotes from Everest," [online], 8 October 2003. Available from Internet: *http://www.mnteverest.net*.

145

Leader Guide

This leader guide will help you facilitate seven small-group sessions for the study of *Vertically Inclined*. The group sessions (Climbing Together) are designed to be approximately one hour in length, but feel free to adapt these sessions to meet the needs of your group and the length of your sessions.

Commit this study to God in prayer, asking Him to put together the small group He desires to participate. Begin your publicity at least six weeks in advance. Send personal invitations to church leaders and others you feel led to contact. Announce the study in the church newsletter, worship bulletin, and on hallway bulletin boards. Secure child care for each session.

Before each session, arrange for a TV-DVD in your meeting room. Preview each video and complete your viewer guide before the session. Also complete the daily study material for the week to prepare you to facilitate and participate in group discussion. Have on hand an attendance sheet, extra Bibles, pens or pencils, and member books. For the first couple of sessions, supply name tags. The Gearing Up section for each small-group session will list other specific items you need to gather for that week's study. This study does not require an introductory session. Distribute member books in small-group session 1.

Begin praying now—and continue praying throughout the study—that God will use this time to do a mighty work in the hearts of group members as they seek to climb upward and forever upward with God.

Session 1

Gearing Up
1. **Pray in preparation for your first small-group session.**
2. **Gather a marker board, chalkboard, or tear sheets.**

Climbing Together
1. As participants arrive, direct them to sign the attendance sheet, prepare a name tag, and pick up a copy of the member book.
2. You may introduce the study by showing the special DVD music video, featuring Brian Doerksen's song, "I Lift My Eyes Up."
3. Introduce yourself and ask group members to do the same. Then ask them to share what they find appealing about this study. List responses on tear sheets, a chalkboard, or a marker board.
4. Read Introduction: Seven Summits (p. 5). Ask the group to turn to the Contents page (p. 3). Review the seven summits of the study. Select volunteers to read aloud About the Study (pp. 6-7). Invite participants to turn through the pages of Summit 1 as the volunteers read about the icons representing daily lessons, High Points, Climbing Gear, and Viewpoints.
5. Explain the value of completing the learning activities (in bold print) to reinforce what they learn through the content. Since many of these activities involve reading Scripture passages in their own Bibles, draw attention to the fact that they will be studying God's Word as they learn.
6. Ask the group to turn to the overview of the first summit on page 8. Ask a volunteer to read the definition of *anticipate* and the summary of Summit 1 Base Camp.
7. Ask a volunteer to read the Memory Pack (memory verse) for summit 1 at the bottom of page 8. Ask participants to turn to page 158. Invite them to cut out each week's Memory Pack and post it in a prominent location or carry it with them in a purse or pocket. Encourage them to read this verse frequently during the week, highlight the key words or phrases, and say it to a family member or friend until they can repeat it from memory.
8. Ask participants to turn to the Base Camp viewer guide for summit 1 (p. 9). Encourage them to take notes and fill in the blanks as they view the video.
9. Play the session 1 video. Review the responses to the Base Camp guide, asking appropriate questions and providing answers to the fill-in-the-blank questions.
10. Assign summit 1 lessons in the member book for discussion at the next Base Camp group session.
11. If members are paying for their books, collect money or explain the procedure for collecting money.
12. Close by praying for openness to God as He teaches you how to climb higher with Him.

Session 2

Gearing Up
Pray in preparation for your small-group session.

Climbing Together

1. Ask members to sign the attendance sheet and wear a name tag (optional).
2. Recite together this week's Memory Pack verse, Isaiah 26:8. Ask, *What does it mean to "wait" on God?*
3. Review Summit 1 Base Camp viewer guide by asking someone to explain the ways God moves. Ask, *Why is it important to be on the lookout for Him?*
4. Guide discussion of this week's study by leading group members to answer these questions or follow these instructions:
   Day 1: *Have you ever been to the mountains? What do the mountains teach us about God?* Explain the concepts of God's transcendence and immanence (p. 11). *What was your response to the Climbing Gear activity on page 13?*
   Day 2: *What response did you check for the question on page 17? Can you think of a time when you saw God do something awesome and unexpected? What was your reaction to the James Fordyce quote on page 15?*
   Day 3: *Without looking, can you remember the four synonyms for the word* wait? (p. 20) Read Isaiah 30:18 together. *How do you feel when you consider the great longing God has for you?* Discuss the C.S. Lewis quote on page 19.
   Day 4: *How does being on the lookout for the little "c" comings of Christ prepare us for His return? What does a constant attitude of expectancy and preparedness involve?* (p. 24) *What happened when you kept watch?* (p. 25)
   Day 5: *In what places might you expect to meet God? What was your response to the first learning activity on page 29?*
5. Say, *On the Mount of Anticipation we learn that godward climbers anticipate an encounter with Christ.* Guide participants to break into groups of two or three for a time of prayer, thanking God for His anticipation of them and asking Him to help them anticipate Him more.
6. Direct participants to the Base Camp viewer guide on page 31. Play the session 2 video. Review the responses to the Base Camp guide.
7. Assign summit 2 for the next group session. Close with prayer. Ask God to help members understand how to be loyal.

Session 3

Gearing Up
Pray in preparation for your small-group session.

Climbing Together

1. Begin with a check-in time to review members' progress on completing daily lessons. Encourage them to keep up with their reading and learning activities.

2. Say together this week's memory verse, Proverbs 3:3. Ask, *What does it mean to have love and faithfulness bound around your neck and written on the tablet of your heart?*

3. Review the Summit 2 Base Camp viewer guide by having someone explain the Mount of Allegiance. Say, *God asks us the same three questions He asked the Israelites. Have you been confronted this week with a situation where you had to choose to follow, depend, or believe?*

4. Guide discussion of this week's study by leading group members to answer these questions or follow these instructions:
   Day 1: *What is a covenant? What's unique about God's covenant with us?* Discuss the meaning of loyalty. (p. 32)
   Day 2: *How are the new and old covenants the same, and how are they different? How does God demonstrate His loyal love toward us? What is your reaction to the William Barclay quote on page 39?*
   Day 3: *What guarantee does God give that His commitment to us is forever? In the learning activity on page 41 what impresses you most about His faithfulness?* Review the "Making the Commitment" Climbing Gear on page 43. Explain that you will be available after the session to talk with anyone who wants to make a commitment to Jesus.
   Day 4: *How did you respond to the first learning activity on page 44? What does true loyalty to Christ involve?* Share your illustration on page 46 and explain how to build a rock-solid love relationship with God.
   Day 5: Explain the significance of a standard (p. 49). *How do we make God our banner? In what areas do you need to work on being more loyal to Him?*

5. Say, *On the Mount of Allegiance we learn that godward climbers are loyal to His standard.* Guide participants in a time of prayer, thanking God for His loyalty and asking Him to help them be loyal in return.

6. Direct participants to the Base Camp viewer guide on page 53. Play the session 3 video. Review the responses to the Base Camp guide.

7. Assign summit 3 for the next group session. Close with prayer. Ask God to help participants align themselves with the humble heart of Christ.

Session 4

Gearing Up
Pray in preparation for your small-group session.

Climbing Together

1. Assign groups of two or three to review the key points of summits 1–3. Suggest that they refer to the overview page of each week. Have members discuss which summit they find the most challenging personally. Allow five minutes for discussion.

2. Say together this week's memory verse, 1 Peter 5:5-6. Ask, *Why does God oppose the proud?*

3. Review Summit 3 Base Camp viewer guide by asking someone to explain the significance of High Places. Ask, *How does being a stargazer help us make our way through high places?*

4. Guide discussion of this week's study by leading group members to answer these questions or follow these instructions:
   Day 1: *What are some symptoms of spiritual high altitude illness?* (p. 54) *How did you define a high place? An idol?* (p. 56) *In the Climbing Gear on page 57, which modern-day idols did you identify?*
   Day 2: Describe how adults figuratively play the childhood game, "King-of-the-Castle." Review the attitudes on the chart on page 61. *Which of these attitudes do you struggle with? How did you react to the C.S. Lewis quote on page 61?*

   Day 3: *What did God want Nebuchadnezzar to learn?* (p. 64) *Why is comparison a dangerous habit? How can we tell when we are becoming arrogant?*
   Day 4: *Why did God liken Saul's attitude of arrogance to the evil of idolatry?* (p. 66) *On the chart on page 68, who do you see yourself as being more like—David or Saul?* Discuss the two sides of pride.
   Day 5: Comment on your reaction and responses to the Humility Test on pages 71-73. Discuss the Augustine quote on page 70. *How can we clothe ourselves with humility on an ongoing basis? Describe a circumstance this week in which you needed to swallow your pride and clothe yourself in humility.*

5. Say, *On the Mount of Appraisal, godward climbers evaluate and make adjustments.* Challenge participants to make a habit of checking their altitude, focus, orientation, and point of reference so they may walk in humility. Lead in prayer, asking God to forgive pride and help participants humbly keep their eyes on Jesus.

6. Direct participants to turn to the Base Camp viewer guide on page 75. Play the session 4 video. Review the responses to the Base Camp guide.

7. Assign summit 4 for the next group session. Close with a time of prayer.

Session 5

Gearing Up
Pray in preparation for your small-group session.

Climbing Together

1. Play the special DVD feature interview with Rusty. (Disc 2) Ask, *Is there anything Rusty said that stood out to you?*

2. Say together this week's memory verse, Isaiah 49:13. Ask, *Does this verse encourage you? Why or why not?*

3. Review the precarious perspectives from point one of the summit 4 viewer guide (p. 75). Ask, *Can you think of a situation in which you struggled with one or more of these perspectives?*

4. Guide discussion of this week's study by leading group members to answer these questions or follow these instructions:

   Day 1: *Did it surprise you that prominent biblical figures asked the "why" question? (p. 77). How do you feel about the fact that followers of Christ are destined to suffer? What are some of the giant hills you have faced or are currently facing? How do you respond to the C.S. Lewis quote on page 76?*

   Day 2: *Why is Jesus the champion of suffering? (p. 82) According to 1 Peter 2, what do those who follow His example do when they suffer? (pp. 82-83)*

   Day 3: *How do the fires of trials purify our faith? In the chart on page 87, were you able to identify some gold and slag? When suffering, how does changing the question from "why" to "what" make a difference?*

   Day 4: *Describe your favorite childhood place of refuge. In the learning activity on page 89, which picture metaphor is the most meaningful to you and why? David said, "In my anguish I cried to the Lord and he answered by setting me free." (Ps. 118:5-9,13-14).How does God set us free during times of trouble?*

   Day 5: *Have you ever felt as though you were just surviving from strength to strength? Describe the emotions you felt during that time. Explain the biblical concept of hope. Describe a time when you leaned on a "spider-web" hope and it gave way. How can we put our hope in Christ?*

5. Say, *On the Mount of Affliction godward climbers learn to persevere through difficulty.* Divide members into groups of two or three for small-group prayer. Pray for those who are currently facing difficulties in their lives.

6. Direct participants to turn to the Base Camp viewer guide on page 97. Play the session 5 video. Review the responses to the Base Camp guide.

7. Assign summit 5 for the next group session. Close in prayer, thanking the Lord for His great affection.

Session 6

Gearing Up
1. **Pray in preparation for your small-group session.**
2. **Gather a marker board, chalkboard, or tear sheets.**

Climbing Together
1. On a tear sheet, chalkboard, or marker board, write the heading "Marks of Affection." Ask the group to brainstorm behaviors and attitudes that characterize affection. List their answers.
2. Say together this week's memory verse, 1 John 4:16. Ask, *What does it mean to "live in love"?*
3. Review Summit 5 Base Camp viewer guide by asking someone to describe their experience of being "seized" and "transformed" by the affection of God. Ask, *What was your "first love" behavior toward God like?*
4. Guide discussion of this week's study by leading group members to answer these questions or follow these instructions:
   Day 1: *What is the meaning of the saying: "I've been seized by the power of a great affection"? In the learning activity on page 98, which of John's statements about loving God impacted you and why? Do you agree with the summary statement: "Apart from God we cannot love"? Explain.* (p. 101)
   Day 2: *With regard to love and obedience, would you describe yourself as more of a doer or a feeler? In the learning activity on page 104, what things did you identify as pleasing God? How did Jesus demonstrate His love for God?*
   Day 3: *Why do you think our love for people is the litmus test of our love for God? Ask someone to review the parable of the Good Samaritan and explain what it teaches about love. How did you rate on the neighborliness report card on page 109?*
   Day 4: *What is the Lex Talionis law? Discuss how Jesus fulfilled this law of justice. Can you think of an example of a time when you deserved justice, but someone showed you mercy? Do you struggle with tit-for-tat behavior? How can you triumph over this type of behavior?* (p. 113)
   Day 5: *How can you tell if your affection for God is growing? Discuss how believers are like palm and cedar trees.* (p. 115) *What impressed you about these trees? How do we keep our love for God alive?*
5. Say, *Godward climbers keep their love alive.* Lead in prayer asking God to sustain and increase your affection for Him.
6. Direct participants to turn to the Base Camp viewer guide on page 119. Play the session 6 video. Review the responses to the Base Camp guide.
7. Assign summit 6 for the next group session. Close in prayer.

Session 7

Gearing Up
1. Pray in preparation for your last small-group session.

Climbing Together

1. Review the Seven Summits on page 142. Ask, *Which summit has impacted you the most and why?*

2. Say together this week's memory verse, Psalm 36:8-9. Ask, *What image comes to mind when you think about the abundance of God's house?*

3. Review Summit 6 Base Camp Viewer Guide by asking someone to review the extravagant inheritance we have in Christ. Ask, *What part of this inheritance means the most to you and why?*

4. Guide discussion of this week's study by leading group members to answer these questions or follow these instructions:
   Day 1: *In the learning activity on page 121, what has the Father given His Son, Jesus? How is Jesus a "chip off the old rock"? (p. 122) Explain what you think is meant by the term, "the fullness of God."*
   Day 2: *Define the word* grace. Discuss the "grace-hold" of God. *How did you answer the final learning activity of day 2? (p. 127)*
   Day 3: Explain what a blessing is. *The pictures you drew on page 129 depicted the abundance of the blessings God has given you. Can you think of another illustration to describe the quantity of what you have received?* Discuss the concept of the "now and not yet." *What does this concept mean for you on a daily basis?*

   Day 4: *What would you do with millions of dollars? Discuss the difference between Mount Bashan and Mount Zion (High Point, page 133). What lesson does this teach us? In the learning activity on pages 133-134, which three riches would you like to experience more?*
   Day 5: *According to Philippians 3:13-14, what is the ultimate goal? What were the believers in Rome told they would see on Mount Zion? What is Mount Zion? What do you think Mary meant by the statement, "The fulfillment of every desire is found in Christ"? How can we keep our eyes on the prize?*

5. Say, *The summit we studied this week encourages us to experience and anticipate the abundance of God. The Mount of Adventure challenges us to press upward and forever upward.* Explain that the last video talks about this challenge. Direct participants to the Base Camp viewer guide on page 140. Play the session 7 video. Review the responses to the Base Camp guide.

6. Spend time in small groups praying that members will pursue the life-long adventure of climbing higher with God.

7. Give members an opportunity to express thanks for the study and for one another.

8. Show the special DVD music video, featuring Brian Doerksen's song, "I Lift My Eyes Up." Close in prayer and dismiss.

153